D1030976

Yes, you squashed cabbage leaf, you disgrace to the noble architecture of these columns, you incarnate insult to the English language: I could pass you off as the Queen of Sheba.

PYGMALION
Act I

PYGMALION

A ROMANCE IN FIVE ACTS

George Bernard Shaw

with Connections

HOLT, RINEHART AND WINSTON
Harcourt Brace & Company

Austin • New York • Orlando • Atlanta • San Francisco
Boston • Dallas • Toronto • London

This edition of *Pygmalion: A Romance in Five Acts* is published by
Holt, Rinehart and Winston as part of the HRW Classics Library.

Cover illustration by Kent Barton.

Requests for permission to make copies of any part of the work should be
mailed to the following address: Permissions Department, Holt, Rinehart
and Winston, 1120 South Capital of Texas Highway, Austin, Texas
78746-6487.

**For permission to reprint copyrighted material, grateful
acknowledgment is made to the following sources:**

Georges Borchardt, Inc.: From "Speaking Across the Divide" by John Lahr
from *The New Yorker,* January 27, 1997. Copyright © 1997 by John Lahr.
Estate of Alan Jay Lerner: From *My Fair Lady: A Musical Play in Two Acts*
by Alan Jay Lerner and Frederick Loewe. Copyright © 1956 by Alan Jay
Lerner and Frederick Loewe.
Little, Brown and Company: "Pygmalion and Galatea" from *Mythology* by
Edith Hamilton. Copyright 1942 by Edith Hamilton.

Printed in the United States of America

ISBN 0-03-053299-X   1 2 3 4 5 6 043 01 00 99 98

CONTENTS

George Bernard Shaw
(1856–1950)

Bernard Shaw (who disliked his first name) described himself as "an upstart son of an alcoholic downstart." Though he came from a Dublin family with claims to a certain position in society, his father's failings led to the family's loss of status, and Shaw was made to feel like an outsider. He decided that he would "show them" by succeeding in the arts.

When he was sixteen, the family broke up, and his mother, whose one concern in life seemed to be her singing, went with her two daughters to London, where she taught music. After four years spent working at various uncongenial jobs (including that of rent collector), Shaw also went to London. He lived with his mother as a rather unwelcome boarder until, at age forty-two, he married. "I did not throw myself into the struggle for life," he was to say later; "I threw my mother into it."

The first nine years in London were bitter and discouraging. Believing that he was meant to be a writer, Shaw haunted museums and concert halls and read omnivorously in an attempt to educate himself. In six years he wrote five novels, all of which were rejected by London publishing houses.

At this time, Shaw also began to write reviews of music, art, books, and drama—brilliant reviews that are still relevant and thought provoking. For most of what he saw in the theater, Shaw had nothing but contempt. Looking back in 1933, he wrote,

> In 1899 the London stage had come into shattering collision with the Norwegian giant, Ibsen. I say "shattering" advisedly because nobody could follow up Ibsen. He

knocked the fashionable drama of the day out of countenance without effectively replacing it, because his plays could never be forced on the London theater for more than a fortnight at a time.

In many countries at this time, there was a growing dissatisfaction with "fashionable drama," which seemed to have little or no relationship to the issues of the day. On the European continent small theaters were being established to present a new kind of drama: in France, the Théâtre-Libre (Free Theater, 1887); in Germany, the Freie Bühne (Free Stage, 1889); in Russia, the Moscow Academic Art Theater (1898).

In England in 1891, J. T. Grein, a young drama critic, started the Independent Theater "for the presentment of real human life." Grein's first production was Henrik Ibsen's shocking exposé of the cost of respectability, *Ghosts. Ghosts* raised a furor in the press but also had defenders, among them Bernard Shaw. Grein looked to the English playwrights for the kinds of plays he wanted to produce, but he found none until Shaw, wishing to prove his own claim that the so-called New Drama was ready to burst forth on the British stage, hastily completed a play he had begun several years earlier. *Widowers' Houses,* an attack on slum landlords, was produced by Grein and was first presented in 1892. Its excoriating criticism of social evils was true to Shaw's belief that art does not exist for art's sake. Art, he believed, should be didactic, and it should serve to reform.

This belief tends to make Shaw sound like a dull and chilly preacher, and in fact he has been accused of lacking human passion. What he did *not* lack was a passionate humanitarianism, which for him transcended romance and idealism. For Shaw, love does not conquer all or solve all of life's problems, as it does in most Victorian plays.

And Shaw had wit and a comic eye. His plays are anything but dull. He accomplished his "teaching" in delightful, mischievous comedies that turn things topsy-turvy and debunk one conventional idea after another. Shaw makes us question absolutes and do some hard thinking. For example, in *Major Barbara* (1905), Barbara, a Salvation Army officer, scorns the wealth her father has earned by manufacturing munitions only to find that this same wealth supports her Salvation Army work. In *Arms and the Man* (1894), Shaw deflates the heroic concept of the soldier. His soldier does not carry a gun. Rather, he carries chocolates because he believes that it is more realistic to worry about being hungry than to worry about being killed.

Shaw's art is the art of anticlimax. He leads us to expect a conventional conclusion and then pulls the rug out from under us, in the process giving us new insights. *Candida* (1897), one of his most delightful and popular plays, is basically a domestic comedy that owes something to Ibsen's *A Doll's House* (1879). Candida, a warm and charming woman in her thirties, is married to a rigid, unimaginative minister. She is also being wooed by a flamboyant, romantic young poet who is forever throwing himself at her feet, begging her to run away with him. In the end, Candida (the "honest" one) says she will choose the weaker man, the one who needs her more. (Presenting a Victorian wife as able to make such a choice was in itself remarkable.) When Candida surprisingly chooses her apparently self-sufficient husband, Shaw makes us reconsider the husband's supposed strength. At the same time, Shaw makes one of his favorite points, that the artist stands alone, strong in power and talent.

In his long life, Shaw wrote more than fifty plays of a variety and a quality matched only by Shakespeare. Sometimes the work of reformists dates badly, as the targets of their criticism disappear. This has not been so with Shaw. With the exception of plays like *Widowers' Houses* and *Fanny's First Play*, Shaw's dramas have held up well and are constantly revived. At the Theater Guild, an American theater company that presented most of Shaw's American premières, the saying always was "When in doubt, do Shaw." In 1925, Shaw's achievements earned him the Nobel Prize in literature.

Shaw remains popular for a variety of reasons: In most cases, the evils and follies he attacked are still with us; the manner in which he launched his attacks is brilliant and witty; and he created some extraordinary parts for actors, especially for women. Shaw wrote most of his great parts for the leading actresses of his day—Janet Achurch, Ellen Terry, and Mrs. Patrick Campbell. (With Terry and Campbell he carried on lengthy epistolary love affairs; according to Shaw, these were the best kind.) To this day, actresses relish playing Shaw's Saint Joan, Eliza Doolittle, Candida, Cleopatra, and Barbara.

In his later years, after *Heartbreak House* (1920) and his greatest play, *Saint Joan* (1923), Shaw wrote such plays as *The Apple Cart* (1929) and *The Millionairess* (1936), which are little more than discussions, opportunities for the playwright to present and argue ideas that interested him. In these later years, Shaw continued to write about his favorite subjects: marriage and religion. In 1950, the year he died, he wrote yet another play, *Why She Would Not*.

Toward the end of his life, as the world seemed determined to destroy itself, Shaw looked on in horror. But he was still the reformer who saw human life as a comedy, not a tragedy. As the apostle of reason, Shaw lived and wrote for the day when all of society could be brought to its senses through reason. In the Epilogue to *Saint Joan*, the soldier asks a question that might have been Shaw's prayer:

> Oh, God, that madest this beautiful earth,
> when will it be ready to receive Thy saints?
> How long, oh Lord, how long?

Preface

A Professor of Phonetics[1]

Shaw stipulated that the text of Pygmalion *be reprinted exactly as he wrote it; this means that the British spelling style is retained, and apostrophes are often omitted, as are periods after abbreviations like* Mrs. *and* Mr. *Shaw's will also requires that each time* Pygmalion *is reprinted, the Preface and the Epilogue be reprinted also.*

As will be seen later on, Pygmalion needs, not a preface, but a sequel, which I have supplied in its due place.

The English have no respect for their language, and will not teach their children to speak it. They cannot spell it because they have nothing to spell it with but an old foreign alphabet of which only the consonants—and not all of them—have any agreed speech value. Consequently no man can teach himself what it should sound like from reading it; and it is impossible for an Englishman to open his mouth without making some other Englishman despise him. Most European languages are now accessible in black and white to foreigners: English and French are not thus accessible even to Englishmen and Frenchmen. The reformer we need most today is an energetic phonetic enthusiast: that is why I have made such a one the hero of a popular play.

There have been heroes of that kind crying in the wilderness for many years past. When I became interested in the subject towards the end of the eighteen-seventies, the illustrious Alexander Melville Bell, the inventor of Visible Speech,[2] had emigrated to Canada, where his son invented the tele-

---

1. **phonetics** (fō·net´iks): the study of speech sounds, their production, and their representation by written symbols.
2. **Visible Speech:** system of symbols that show the position of the throat, tongue, and lips in making sounds.

phone; but Alexander J. Ellis was still a London patriarch, with an impressive head always covered by a velvet skull cap, for which he would apologize to public meetings in a very courtly manner. He and Tito Pagliardini, another phonetic veteran, were men whom it was impossible to dislike. Henry Sweet, then a young man, lacked their sweetness of character: he was about as conciliatory to conventional mortals as Ibsen or Samuel Butler.[3] His great ability as a phonetician (he was, I think, the best of them all at his job) would have entitled him to high official recognition, and perhaps enabled him to popularize his subject, but for his Satanic contempt for all academic dignitaries and persons in general who thought more of Greek than of phonetics. Once, in the days when the Imperial Institute rose in South Kensington, and Joseph Chamberlain[4] was booming the Empire, I induced the editor of a leading monthly review to commission an article from Sweet on the imperial importance of his subject. When it arrived, it contained nothing but a savagely derisive attack on a professor of language and literature whose chair Sweet regarded as proper to a phonetic expert only. The article, being libellous, had to be returned as impossible; and I had to renounce my dream of dragging its author into the limelight. When I met him afterwards, for the first time for many years, I found to my astonishment that he, who had been a quite tolerably presentable young man, had actually managed by sheer scorn to alter his personal appearance until he had become a sort of walking repudiation of Oxford and all its traditions. It must have been largely in his own despite that he was squeezed into something called a Readership of phonetics there. The future of phonetics rests probably with his pupils, who all swore by him; but nothing could bring the man himself into any sort of compliance with

---

3. **Samuel Butler** (1835–1902): English writer who satirized Victorian society in his books and essays.
4. **Joseph Chamberlain** (1836–1914): British colonial secretary from 1895 to 1903.

the university to which he nevertheless clung by divine right in an intensely Oxonian way. I daresay his papers, if he has left any, include some satires that may be published without too destructive results fifty years hence. He was, I believe, not in the least an ill-natured man: very much the opposite, I should say; but he would not suffer fools gladly; and to him all scholars who were not rabid phoneticians were fools.

Those who knew him will recognize in my third act the allusion to the Current Shorthand in which he used to write postcards. It may be acquired from a four and sixpenny manual published by the Clarendon Press. The postcards which Mrs Higgins describes are such as I have received from Sweet. I would decipher a sound which a cockney would represent by *zerr*, and a Frenchman by *seu*, and then write demanding with some heat what on earth it meant. Sweet, with boundless contempt for my stupidity, would reply that it not only meant but obviously was the word Result, as no other word containing that sound, and capable of making sense with the context, existed in any language spoken on earth. That less expert mortals should require fuller indications was beyond Sweet's patience. Therefore, though the whole point of his Current Shorthand is that it can express every sound in the language perfectly, vowels as well as consonants, and that your hand has to make no stroke except the easy and current ones with which you write m, n, and u, l, p, and q, scribbling them at whatever angle comes easiest to you, his unfortunate determination to make this remarkable and quite legible script serve also as a shorthand reduced it in his own practice to the most inscrutable of cryptograms. His true objective was the provision of a full, accurate, legible script for our language; but he was led past that by his contempt for the popular Pitman system of shorthand, which he called the Pitfall system. The triumph of Pitman was a triumph of business organization: there was a weekly paper to persuade you to learn Pitman: there were cheap textbooks and exercise books and transcripts of speeches for you to copy, and schools where experienced teachers coached you up to the necessary proficiency. Sweet could not organize his market in that fashion. He might as well have been the Sybil[5] who tore up the leaves of prophecy that nobody would attend to. The four and sixpenny manual, mostly in his lithographed handwriting, that was never vulgarly[6] advertized, may perhaps some day be taken up by a syndicate and pushed upon the public as The Times pushed the Encyclopædia Britannica; but until then it will certainly not prevail against Pitman. I have bought three copies of it during my lifetime; and I am informed by the publishers that its cloistered existence is still a steady and healthy one. I actually learned the system two several[7] times; and yet the shorthand in which I am writing these lines is Pitman's. And the reason is, that my secretary cannot transcribe Sweet, having been perforce taught in the schools of Pitman. In America I could use the commercially organized Gregg shorthand, which has taken a hint from Sweet by making its letters writable (current, Sweet would have called them) instead of having to be geometrically drawn like Pitman's; but all these systems, including Sweet's, are spoilt by making them available for verbatim reporting, in which complete and exact spelling and word division are impossible. A complete and exact phonetic script is neither practicable nor necessary for ordinary use; but if we enlarge our alphabet to the Russian size, and make our spelling as phonetic as Spanish, the advance will be prodigious.

Pygmalion Higgins is not a portrait of Sweet, to whom the adventure of Eliza Doolittle would have been impossible; still, as will be seen, there are touches of Sweet in the play. With Higgins's physique and temperament Sweet might have set the Thames on fire. As it was, he impressed himself professionally on Europe to an extent that made his comparative personal obscurity, and the failure of Oxford to do justice

---

5. **Sybil:** female prophet. The usual spelling of the word is *sibyl*.
6. **vulgarly:** popularly.
7. **several:** different.

to his eminence, a puzzle to foreign specialists in his subject. I do not blame Oxford, because I think Oxford is quite right in demanding a certain social amenity from its nurslings (heaven knows it is not exorbitant in its requirements!); for although I well know how hard it is for a man of genius with a seriously underrated subject to maintain serene and kindly relations with the men who underrate it, and who keep all the best places for less important subjects which they profess without originality and sometimes without much capacity for them, still, if he overwhelms them with wrath and disdain, he cannot expect them to heap honors on him.

Of the later generations of phoneticians I know little. Among them towered Robert Bridges, to whom perhaps Higgins may owe his Miltonic[8] sympathies, though here again I must disclaim all portraiture. But if the play makes the public aware that there are such people as phoneticians, and that they are among the most important people in England at present, it will serve its turn.

I wish to boast that Pygmalion has been an extremely successful play, both on stage and screen, all over Europe and North America as well as at home. It is so intensely and deliberately didactic, and its subject is esteemed so dry, that I delight in throwing it at the heads of the wiseacres who repeat the parrot cry that art should never be didactic. It goes to prove my contention that great art can never be anything else.

Finally, and for the encouragement of people troubled with accents that cut them off from all high employment, I may add that the change wrought by Professor Higgins in the flower girl is neither impossible nor uncommon. The modern concierge's daughter who fulfils her ambition by playing the Queen of Spain in Ruy Blas at the Théâtre Français is only one of many thousands of men and women who have sloughed off their native dialects and acquired a new tongue. Our West End shop assistants and domestic servants are bi-lingual. But

---

8. **Miltonic:** relating to the English poet John Milton (1608–1674).

the thing has to be done scientifically, or the last state of the aspirant may be worse than the first. An honest slum dialect is more tolerable than the attempts of phonetically untaught persons to imitate the plutocracy. Ambitious flower girls who read this play must not imagine that they can pass themselves off as fine ladies by untutored imitation. They must learn their alphabet over again, and differently, from a phonetic expert. Imitation will only make them ridiculous.

Note for Technicians. A complete representation of the play as printed for the first time in this edition is technically possible only on the cinema screen or on stages furnished with exceptionally elaborate machinery. For ordinary theatrical use the scenes separated by rows of asterisks are to be omitted.

In the dialogue an *e* upside down[9] indicates the indefinite vowel, something called obscure or neutral, for which, though it is one of the commonest sounds in English speech, our wretched alphabet has no letter.

---

9. *e* **upside down:** Shaw is referring to the schwa (ə), used in dictionaries to represent such sounds as that of the initial *a* in *again*, *e* in *parent*, *i* in *vanity*, *o* in *compare*, and *u* in *focus*.

Characters

ELIZA DOOLITTLE

HENRY HIGGINS

COLONEL PICKERING

ALFRED DOOLITTLE

MRS HIGGINS

MRS PEARCE

FREDDY EYNSFORD HILL

MRS EYNSFORD HILL

MISS EYNSFORD HILL

COUNT NEPOMMUCK

BYSTANDERS

HOSTESS

HOST

PARLORMAID

TAXIMEN

CONSTABLES

FOOTMEN

Act I

London at 11.15 P.M. Torrents of heavy summer rain. Cab whistles blowing frantically in all directions. Pedestrians running for shelter into the portico of St Paul's church (not Wren's[1] cathedral but Inigo Jones's[2] church in Covent Garden vegetable market), among them a lady and her daughter in evening dress. All are peering out gloomily at the rain, except one man with his back turned to the rest, wholly preoccupied with a notebook in which he is writing.

The church clock strikes the first quarter.

The Daughter (*in the space between the central pillars, close to the one on her left*). I'm getting chilled to the bone. What can Freddy be doing all this time? He's been gone twenty minutes.

The Mother (*on her daughter's right*). Not so long. But he ought to have got us a cab by this.

A Bystander (*on the lady's right*). He wont get no cab not until half-past eleven, missus, when they come back after dropping their theatre fares.

The Mother. But we must have a cab. We cant stand here until half-past eleven. It's too bad.

The Bystander. Well, it aint my fault, missus.

The Daughter. If Freddy had a bit of gumption, he would have got one at the theatre door.

The Mother. What could he have done, poor boy?

The Daughter. Other people got cabs. Why couldnt he?

---

1. **Wren's:** Christopher Wren (1632–1723), an English architect.
2. **Inigo Jones's:** Inigo Jones (1573–1652), another English architect.

9

[FREDDY *rushes in out of the rain from the Southampton Street side, and comes between them closing a dripping umbrella. He is a young man of twenty, in evening dress, very wet round the ankles.*]

The Daughter. Well, havnt you got a cab?

Freddy. Theres not one to be had for love or money.

The Mother. Oh, Freddy, there must be one. You cant have tried.

The Daughter. It's too tiresome. Do you expect us to go and get one ourselves?

Freddy. I tell you theyre all engaged. The rain was so sudden: nobody was prepared; and everybody had to take a cab. Ive been to Charing Cross one way and nearly to Ludgate Circus the other; and they were all engaged.

The Mother. Did you try Trafalgar Square?

Freddy. There wasnt one at Trafalgar Square.

The Daughter. Did you try?

Freddy. I tried as far as Charing Cross Station. Did you expect me to walk to Hammersmith?

The Daughter. You havnt tried at all.

The Mother. You really are very helpless, Freddy. Go again; and dont come back until you have found a cab.

Freddy. I shall simply get soaked for nothing.

The Daughter. And what about us? Are we to stay here all night in this draught,[3] with next to nothing on. You selfish pig—

Freddy. Oh, very well: I'll go, I'll go. (*He opens his umbrella and dashes off Strandwards, but comes into collision with a flower girl who is hurrying in for shelter, knocking her basket out of her hands. A blinding flash of lightning, followed instantly by a rattling peal of thunder, orchestrates the incident*).

The Flower Girl. Nah then, Freddy: look wh' y' gowin, deah.

Freddy. Sorry. (*He rushes off*).

The Flower Girl (*picking up her scattered flowers and replacing them in the basket*). Theres menners f' yer! Tə-oo banches

---

3. **draught:** British spelling of *draft.*

o voylets trod into the mad.[4] (*She sits down on the plinth[5] of the column, sorting her flowers, on the lady's right. She is not at all a romantic figure. She is perhaps eighteen, perhaps twenty, hardly older. She wears a little sailor hat of black straw that has long been exposed to the dust and soot of London and has seldom if ever been brushed. Her hair needs washing rather badly: its mousy color can hardly be natural. She wears a shoddy black coat that reaches nearly to her knees and is shaped to her waist. She has a brown skirt with a coarse apron. Her boots are much the worse for wear. She is no doubt as clean as she can afford to be; but compared to the ladies she is very dirty. Her features are no worse than theirs, but their condition leaves something to be desired; and she needs the services of a dentist*).

The Mother. How do you know that my son's name is Freddy, pray?

The Flower Girl. Ow, eez yə-ooa san, is e? Wal, fewd dan y' də-ooty bawmz a mather should, eed now bettern to spawl a pore gel's flahrzn than ran awy athaht pyin. Will ye-oo py me f'them?[6] (*Here, with apologies, this desperate attempt to represent her dialect without a phonetic alphabet must be abandoned as unintelligible outside London*).

The Daughter. Do nothing of the sort, mother. The idea!

The Mother. Please allow me, Clara. Have you any pennies?

The Daughter. No. Ive nothing smaller than sixpence.

The Flower Girl (*hopefully*). I can give you change for a tanner,[7] kind lady.

The Mother (*to* CLARA). Give it to me. (CLARA *parts reluctantly*). Now (*to the girl*). This is for your flowers.

The Flower Girl. Thank you kindly, lady.

---

4. **There's . . . mad:** "There's manners for you! Two bunches of violets trod into the mud."
5. **plinth:** square block at the base of a column.
6. **Ow . . . f'them:** "Oh, he's your son, is he? Well, if you'd done your duty by him as a mother should, he'd know better than to spoil a poor girl's flowers and then run away without paying. Will you pay me for them?"
7. **tanner:** British slang for "sixpence."

The Daughter. Make her give you the change. These things are only a penny a bunch.

The Mother. Do hold your tongue, Clara. (*To the girl*) You can keep the change.

The Flower Girl. Oh, thank you, lady.

The Mother. Now tell me how you know that young gentleman's name.

The Flower Girl. I didnt.

The Mother. I heard you call him by it. Dont try to deceive me.

The Flower Girl (*protesting*). Who's trying to deceive you? I called him Freddy or Charlie same as you might yourself if you was talking to a stranger and wished to be pleasant.

The Daughter. Sixpence thrown away! Really, mamma, you might have spared Freddy that. (*She retreats in disgust behind the pillar*).

[*An elderly gentleman of the amiable military type rushes into the shelter, and closes a dripping umbrella. He is in the same plight as* FREDDY, *very wet about the ankles. He is in evening dress, with a light overcoat. He takes the place left vacant by the daughter.*]

The Gentleman. Phew!

The Mother (*to the gentleman*). Oh, sir, is there any sign of its stopping?

The Gentleman. I'm afraid not. It started worse than ever about two minutes ago. (*He goes to the plinth beside the flower girl; puts up his foot on it; and stoops to turn down his trouser ends*).

The Mother. Oh dear! (*She retires sadly and joins her daughter*).

The Flower Girl (*taking advantage of the military gentleman's proximity to establish friendly relations with him*). If it's worse, it's a sign it's nearly over. So cheer up, Captain; and buy a flower off a poor girl.

The Gentleman. I'm sorry, I havnt any change.

The Flower Girl. I can give you change, Captain.

The Gentleman. For a sovereign? Ive nothing less.

The Flower Girl. Garn! Oh do buy a flower off me, Captain. I can change half-a-crown. Take this for tuppence.

The Gentleman. Now dont be troublesome: theres a good girl. (*Trying his pockets*) I really havnt any change—Stop: heres three halfpence, if thats any use to you. (*He retreats to the other pillar*).

The Flower Girl (*disappointed, but thinking three halfpence better than nothing*). Thank you, sir.

The Bystander (*to the girl*). You be careful: give him a flower for it. Theres a bloke here behind taking down every blessed word youre saying. (*All turn to the man who is taking notes*).

The Flower Girl (*springing up terrified*). I aint done nothing wrong by speaking to the gentleman. Ive a right to sell flowers if I keep off the kerb.[8] (*Hysterically*) I'm a respectable girl: so help me, I never spoke to him except to ask him to buy a flower off me.

[*General hubbub, mostly sympathetic to the flower girl , but deprecating her excessive sensibility. Cries of* Dont start hollerin. Who's hurting you? Nobody's going to touch you. Whats the good of fussing? Steady on. Easy, easy, *etc., come from the elderly staid spectators, who pat her comfortingly. Less patient ones bid her shut her head, or ask her roughly what is wrong with her. A remoter group, not knowing what the matter is, crowd in and increase the noise with question and answer:* Whats the row? What-she do? Where is he? A tec[9] taking her down. What! him? Yes: him over there: Took money off the gentleman, *etc.*]

The Flower Girl (*breaking through them to the gentleman, crying wildly*). Oh, sir, dont let him charge me. You dunno what it means to me. Theyll take away my character and drive me on the streets for speaking to gentlemen. They—

The Note Taker (*coming forward on her right, the rest crowding after him*). There! there! there! there! who's hurting you, you silly girl? What do you take me for?

---

8. **kerb:** British spelling of *curb.*
9. **tec:** slang for "detective."

The Bystander. It's aw rawt: e's a genleman: look at his bə-oots. (*Explaining to the note taker*) She thought you was a copper's nark, sir.

The Note Taker (*with quick interest*). Whats a copper's nark?

The Bystander (*inapt at definition*). It's a—well, it's a copper's nark, as you might say. What else would you call it? A sort of informer.

The Flower Girl (*still hysterical*). I take my Bible oath I never said a word—

The Note Taker (*overbearing but good-humored*). Oh, shut up, shut up. Do I look like a policeman?

The Flower Girl (*far from reassured*). Then what did you take down my words for? How do I know whether you took me down right? You just shew[10] me what youve wrote about me. (*The note taker opens his book and holds it steadily under her nose, though the pressure of the mob trying to read it over his shoulders would upset a weaker man*). Whats that? That aint proper writing. I cant read that.

The Note Taker. I can. (*Reads, reproducing her pronunciation exactly*) "Cheer ap, Keptin; n' baw ya flahr orf a pore gel."

The Flower Girl (*much distressed*). It's because I called him Captain. I meant no harm. (*To the gentleman*) Oh, sir, dont let him lay a charge agen me for a word like that. You—

The Gentleman. Charge! I make no charge. (*To the note taker*) Really, sir, if you are a detective, you need not begin protecting me against molestation by young women until I ask you. Anybody could see that the girl meant no harm.

The Bystanders Generally (*demonstrating against police espionage*). Course they could. What business is it of yours? You mind your own affairs. He wants promotion, he does. Taking down people's words! Girl never said a word to him. What harm if she did? Nice thing a girl cant shelter from the rain without being insulted, *etc., etc., etc.* (*She is conducted by the more sympathetic demonstrators back to her plinth, where she resumes her seat and struggles with her emotion*).

---

10. **shew:** archaic spelling of *show*.

The Bystander. He aint a tec. Hes a blooming busybody: thats what he is. I tell you, look at his bə-oots.

The Note Taker (*turning on him genially*). And how are all your people down at Selsey?

The Bystander (*suspiciously*). Who told you my people come from Selsey?

The Note Taker. Never you mind. They did. (*To the girl*) How do you come to be up so far east? You were born in Lisson Grove.

The Flower Girl (*appalled*). Oh, what harm is there in my leaving Lisson Grove? It wasnt fit for a pig to live in; and I had to pay four-and-six a week. (*In tears*) Oh, boo—hoo—oo—

The Note Taker. Live where you like; but stop that noise.

The Gentleman (*to the girl*). Come, come! he cant touch you: you have a right to live where you please.

A Sarcastic Bystander (*thrusting himself between the note taker and the gentleman*). Park Lane, for instance. I'd like to go into the Housing Question with you, I would.

The Flower Girl (*subsiding into a brooding melancholy over her basket, and talking very low-spiritedly to herself*). I'm a good girl, I am.

The Sarcastic Bystander (*not attending to her*). Do you know where *I* come from?

The Note Taker (*promptly*). Hoxton.

[*Titterings: Popular interest in the note taker's performance increases.*]

The Sarcastic One (*amazed*). Well, who said I didnt? Bly me! you know everything, you do.

The Flower Girl (*still nursing her sense of injury*). Aint no call to meddle with me, he aint.

The Bystander (*to her*). Of course he aint. Dont you stand it from him. (*To the note taker*) See here: what call have you to know about people what never offered to meddle with you?

The Flower Girl. Let him say what he likes. I dont want to have no truck with him.

The Bystander. You take us for dirt under your feet, dont you? Catch you taking liberties with a gentleman!

The Sarcastic Bystander. Yes: tell him where he come from if you want to go fortune-telling.

The Note Taker. Cheltenham, Harrow, Cambridge, and India.

The Gentleman. Quite right.

[*Great laughter. Reaction in the note taker's favor. Exclamations of* He knows all about it. Told him proper. Hear him tell the toff [11] *where he come from? etc.*]

The Gentleman. May I ask, sir, do you do this for your living at a music hall?

The Note Taker. I've thought of that. Perhaps I shall some day.

[*The rain has stopped; and the persons on the outside of the crowd begin to drop off.*]

The Flower Girl (*resenting the reaction*). He's no gentleman, he aint, to interfere with a poor girl.

The Daughter (*out of patience, pushing her way rudely to the front and displacing the gentleman, who politely retires to the other side of the pillar*). What on earth is Freddy doing? I shall get pneumownia if I stay in this draught any longer.

The Note Taker (*to himself, hastily making a note of her pronunciation of "monia"*). Earlscourt.

The Daughter (*violently*). Will you please keep your impertinent remarks to yourself?

The Note Taker. Did I say that out loud? I didnt mean to. I beg your pardon. Your mother's Epsom, unmistakeably.

The Mother (*advancing between the daughter and the note taker*). How very curious! I was brought up in Largelady Park, near Epsom.

The Note Taker (*uproariously amused*). Ha! ha! What a devil of a name! Excuse me. (*To the daughter*) You want a cab, do you?

The Daughter. Dont dare speak to me.

The Mother. Oh please, please, Clara. (*Her daughter repudiates her with an angry shrug and retires haughtily*). We should be so

---

11. **toff:** British slang for "dandy" or "fop."

grateful to you, sir, if you found us a cab. (*The note taker produces a whistle*). Oh, thank you. (*She joins her daughter*).

[*The note taker blows a piercing blast.*]

The Sarcastic Bystander. There! I knowed he was a plainclothes copper.

The Bystander. That aint a police whistle: thats a sporting whistle.

The Flower Girl (*still preoccupied with her wounded feelings*). He's no right to take away my character. My character is the same to me as any lady's.

The Note Taker. I dont know whether youve noticed it; but the rain stopped about two minutes ago.

The Bystander. So it has. Why didnt you say so before? and us losing our time listening to your silliness! (*He walks off towards the Strand*).

The Sarcastic Bystander. I can tell where you come from. You come from Anwell. Go back there.

The Note Taker (*helpfully*). Hanwell.

The Sarcastic Bystander (*affecting great distinction of speech*). Thenk you, teacher. Haw haw! So long. (*He touches his hat with mock respect and strolls off*).

The Flower Girl. Frightening people like that! How would he like it himself?

The Mother. It's quite fine now, Clara. We can walk to a motor bus. Come. (*She gathers her skirts above her ankles and hurries off towards the Strand*).

The Daughter. But the cab— (*Her mother is out of hearing*). Oh, how tiresome! (*She follows angrily*).

[*All the rest have gone except the note taker, the gentleman, and the flower girl, who sits arranging her basket, and still pitying herself in murmurs.*]

The Flower Girl. Poor girl! Hard enough for her to live without being worried and chivied.[12]

---

12. **worrited and chivied:** worried and tormented.

The Gentleman (*returning to his former place on the note taker's left*). How do you do it, if I may ask?

The Note Taker. Simply phonetics. The science of speech. Thats my profession: also my hobby. Happy is the man who can make a living by his hobby! You can spot an Irishman or a Yorkshireman by his brogue. *I* can place any man within six miles. I can place him within two miles in London. Sometimes within two streets.

The Flower Girl. Ought to be ashamed of himself, unmanly coward!

The Gentleman. But is there a living in that?

The Note Taker. Oh yes. Quite a fat one. This is an age of upstarts. Men begin in Kentish Town with £80 a year, and end in Park Lane with a hundred thousand. They want to drop Kentish Town; but they give themselves away every time they open their mouths. Now I can teach them—

The Flower Girl. Let him mind his own business and leave a poor girl—

The Note Taker (*explosively*). Woman: cease this detestable boohooing instantly; or else seek the shelter of some other place of worship.

The Flower Girl (*with feeble defiance*). Ive a right to be here if I like, same as you.

The Note Taker. A woman who utters such depressing and disgusting sounds has no right to be anywhere—no right to live. Remember that you are a human being with a soul and the divine gift of articulate speech: that your native language is the language of Shakespear and Milton and The Bible; and dont sit there crooning like a bilious pigeon.

The Flower Girl (*quite overwhelmed, looking up at him in mingled wonder and deprecation without daring to raise her head*). Ah-ah-ah-ow-ow-ow-oo!

The Note Taker (*whipping out his book*). Heavens! what a sound! (*He writes; then holds out the book and reads, reproducing her vowels exactly*). Ah-ah-ah-ow-ow-ow-oo!

The Flower Girl (*tickled by the performance, and laughing in spite of herself*). Garn!

The Note Taker. You see this creature with her kerbstone English: the English that will keep her in the gutter to the end of her days. Well, sir, in three months I could pass that girl off as a duchess at an ambassador's garden party. I could even get her a place as lady's maid or shop assistant, which requires better English.

The Flower Girl. What's that you say?

The Note Taker. Yes, you squashed cabbage leaf, you disgrace to the noble architecture of these columns, you incarnate insult to the English language: I could pass you of as the Queen of Sheba. (*To the* GENTLEMAN) Can you believe that?

The Gentleman. Of course I can. I am myself a student of Indian dialects; and—

The Note Taker (*eagerly*). Are you? Do you know Colonel Pickering, the author of Spoken Sanscrit?

The Gentleman. I am Colonel Pickering. Who are you?

The Note Taker. Henry Higgins, author of Higgins's Universal Alphabet.

Pickering (*with enthusiasm*). I came from India to meet you.

Higgins. I was going to India to meet you.

Pickering. Where do you live?

Higgins. 27A Wimpole Street. Come and see me tomorrow.

Pickering. I'm at the Carlton. Come with me now and lets have a jaw over some supper.

Higgins. Right you are.

The Flower Girl (*to* PICKERING, *as he passes her*). Buy a flower, kind gentleman. I'm short for my lodging.

Pickering. I really havnt any change. I'm sorry. (*He goes away*).

Higgins (*shocked at the girl's mendacity*).[13] Liar. You said you could change half-a-crown.

The Flower Girl (*rising in desperation*). You ought to be stuffed with nails, you ought. (*Flinging the basket at his feet*) Take the whole blooming basket for sixpence.

---

13. **mendacity:** deceit.

[*The church clock strikes the second quarter.*]

Higgins (*hearing in it the voice of God, rebuking him for his Pharisaic[14] want of charity to the poor girl*). A reminder. (*He raises his hat solemnly; then throws a handful of money into the basket and follows* PICKERING).

The Flower Girl (*picking up a half-crown*). Ah-ow-ooh! (*Picking up a couple of florins*) Aaah-ow-ooh! (*Picking up several coins*) Aaaaaah-ow-ooh! (*Picking up a half-sovereign*) Aaaaaaaaaaaaah-ow-ooh!!!

Freddy (*springing out of a taxicab*). Got one at last. Hallo! (*To the girl*) Where are the two ladies that were here?

The Flower Girl. They walked to the bus when the rain stopped.

Freddy. And left me with a cab on my hands! Damnation!

The Flower Girl (*with grandeur*). Never you mind, young man. I'm going home in a taxi. (*She sails off to the cab. The driver puts his hand behind him and holds the door firmly shut against her. Quite understanding his mistrust, she shews him her handful of money*). A taxi fare aint no object to me, Charlie. (*He grins and opens the door*). Here. What about the basket?

The Taximan. Give it here. Tuppence extra.

Liza. No: I dont want nobody to see it. (*She crushes it into the cab and gets in, continuing the conversation through the window*). Goodbye, Freddy.

Freddy (*dazedly raising his hat*). Goodbye.

Taximan. Where to?

Liza. Bucknam Pellis [*Buckingham Palace*].

Taximan. What d'ye mean—Bucknam Pellis?

Liza. Dont you know where it is? In the Green Park, where the King lives. Goodbye, Freddy. Dont let me keep you standing there. Goodbye.

Freddy. Goodbye. (*He goes*).

Taximan. Here? Whats this about Bucknam Pellis? What business have you at Bucknam Pellis?

---

14. **Pharisaic** (far´i·sā´ik): hypocritical.

Liza. Of course I havnt none. But I wasnt going to let him know that. You drive me home.

Taximan. And wheres home?

Liza. Angel Court, Drury Lane, next Meiklejohn's oil shop.

Taximan. That sounds more like it, Judy. (*He drives off*).

* * *

Let us follow the taxi to the entrance to Angel Court, a narrow little archway between two shops, one of them Meiklejohn's oil shop. When it stops there, Eliza gets out, dragging her basket with her.

Liza. How much?

Taximan (*indicating the taximeter*). Cant you read? A shilling.

Liza. A shilling for two minutes!!

Taximan. Two minutes or ten: it's all the same.

Liza. Well, I dont call it right.

Taximan. Ever been in a taxi before?

Liza (*with dignity*). Hundreds of thousands of times, young man.

Taximan (*laughing at her*). Good for you, Judy. Keep the shilling, darling, with best love from all at home. Good luck! (*He drives off*).

Liza (*humiliated*). Impidence!

[*She picks up the basket and trudges up the alley with it to her lodging: a small room with very old wall paper hanging loose in the damp places. A broken pane in the window is mended with paper. A portrait of a popular actor and a fashion plate of ladies' dresses, all wildly beyond poor* ELIZA's *means, both torn from newspapers, are pinned up on the wall. A birdcage hangs in the window; but its tenant died long ago: It remains as a memorial only.*

These are the only visible luxuries: the rest is the irreducible minimum of poverty's needs: a wretched bed heaped with all sorts of coverings that have any warmth in them, a draped packing case with a basin and jug on it and a little looking glass over it, a chair and table, the refuse of some suburban kitchen, and an American alarum clock on the shelf above the unused fireplace: the whole lighted with a gas lamp with a penny in the slot meter. Rent: four shillings a week.]

Here Eliza, chronically weary, but too excited to go to bed, sits, counting her new riches and dreaming and planning what to do with them, until the gas goes out, when she enjoys for the first time the sensation of being able to put in another penny without grudging it. This prodigal mood does not extinguish her gnawing sense of the need for economy sufficiently to prevent her from calculating that she can dream and plan in bed more cheaply and warmly than sitting up without a fire. So she takes off her shawl and skirt and adds them to the miscellaneous bedclothes. Then she kicks off her shoes and gets into bed without any further change.

Act II

Next day at 11 A.M. HIGGINS's *laboratory in Wimpole Street. It is a room on the first floor, looking on the street, and was meant for the drawing room. The double doors are in the middle of the back wall; and persons entering find in the corner to their right two tall file cabinets at right angles to one another against the wall. In this corner stands a flat writing-table, on which are a phonograph, a laryngoscope,[1] a row of tiny organ pipes with a bellows,[2] a set of lamp chimneys for singing flames[3] with burners attached to a gas plug in the wall by an indiarubber tube, several tuning-forks of different sizes, a life-size image of half a human head, shewing in section the vocal organs, and a box containing a supply of wax cylinders for the phonograph.*

Further down the room, on the same side, is a fireplace, with a comfortable leather-covered easy-chair at the side of the hearth nearest the door, and a coal-scuttle. There is a clock on the mantelpiece. Between the fireplace and the phonograph table is a stand for newspapers.

On the other side of the central door, to the left of the visitor, is a cabinet of shallow drawers. On it is a telephone and the telephone directory. The corner beyond, and most of the side wall, is occupied by a grand piano, with the keyboard at the end furthest from the door, and a bench for the player extending the full length of the keyboard. On the piano is a dessert dish heaped with fruit and sweets, mostly chocolates.

The middle of the room is clear. Besides the easy-chair, the piano bench, and two chairs at the phonograph table, there is one stray

---

1. **laryngoscope** (lə·riŋ´gō·skōp´): instrument for examining the larynx.
2. **bellows:** device that pulls air in and then expels it in a current, used in pipe organs.
3. **singing flames:** flames that produce a musical tone by causing air to vibrate in an open tube held over them.

chair. It stands near the fireplace. On the walls, engravings; mostly Piranesi[4] and mezzotint[5] portraits. No paintings.

PICKERING *is seated at the table, putting down some cards and a tuning-fork which he has been using.* HIGGINS *is standing up near him, closing two or three file drawers which are hanging out. He appears in the morning light as a robust, vital, appetizing sort of man of forty or thereabouts, dressed in a professional-looking black frock-coat with a white linen collar and black silk tie. He is of the energetic, scientific type, heartily, even violently interested in everything that can be studied as a scientific subject, and careless about himself and other people, including their feelings. He is, in fact, but for his years and size, rather like a very impetuous baby "taking notice" eagerly and loudly, and requiring almost as much watching to keep him out of unintended mischief. His manner varies from genial bullying when he is in a good humor to stormy petulance when anything goes wrong; but he is so entirely frank and void of malice that he remains likeable even in his least reasonable moments.*

Higgins (*as he shuts the last drawer*). Well, I think thats the whole show.

Pickering. It's really amazing. I havnt taken half of it in, you know.

Higgins. Would you like to go over any of it again?

Pickering (*rising and coming to the fireplace, where he plants himself with his back to the fire*). No, thank you: not now. I'm quite done up for this morning.

Higgins (*following him, and standing beside him on his left*). Tired of listening to sounds?

Pickering. Yes. It's a fearful strain. I rather fancied myself because I can pronounce twenty-four distinct vowel sounds; but your hundred and thirty beat me. I cant hear a bit of difference between most of them.

---

4. **Piranesi:** works by Giambattista Piranesi (jäm´bät·tē´stä pir´ə·nä´zē) (1720–1778), an Italian artist.
5. **mezzotint** (met´sō·tint´): copper or steel engraving.

Higgins (*chuckling, and going over to the piano to eat sweets*). Oh, that comes with practice. You hear no difference at first; but you keep on listening, and presently you find theyre all as different as A from B. (MRS PEARCE *looks in; she is* HIGGINS's *housekeeper*). Whats the matter?

Mrs Pearce (*hesitating, evidently perplexed*). A young woman asks to see you, sir.

Higgins. A young woman! What does she want?

Mrs Pearce. Well, sir, she says youll be glad to see her when you know what she's come about. She's quite a common girl, sir. Very common indeed. I should have sent her away, only I thought perhaps you wanted her to talk into your machines. I hope Ive not done wrong; but really you see such queer people sometimes—youll excuse me, I'm sure, sir—

Higgins. Oh, thats all right, Mrs Pearce. Has she an interesting accent?

Mrs Pearce. Oh, something dreadful, sir, really. I dont know how you can take an interest in it.

Higgins (*to* PICKERING). Lets have her up. Shew her up, Mrs Pearce (*he rushes across to his working table and picks out a cylinder to use on the phonograph*).

Mrs Pearce (*only half resigned to it*). Very well, sir. It's for you to say. (*She goes downstairs*).

Higgins. This is rather a bit of luck. I'll shew you how I make records. We'll set her talking; and I'll take it down first in Bell's Visible Speech; then in broad Romic; and then we'll get her on the phonograph so that you can turn her on as often as you like with the written transcript before you.

Mrs Pearce (*returning*). This is the young woman, sir.

[*The flower girl enters in state. She has a hat with three ostrich feathers, orange, sky-blue, and red. She has a nearly clean apron and the shoddy coat has been tidied a little. The pathos of this deplorable figure, with its innocent vanity and consequential air, touches* PICKERING, *who has already straightened himself in the presence of* MRS PEARCE. *But as to* HIGGINS, *the only distinction he makes between men and women is that when he is neither bullying*

nor exclaiming to the heavens against some feather-weight cross,[6]
he coaxes women as a child coaxes its nurse when it wants to get
anything out of her.]

Higgins (*brusquely, recognizing her with unconcealed disappoint-*
ment, and at once, babylike, making an intolerable grievance of it).
Why, this is the girl I jotted down last night. She's no use: Ive
got all the records I want of the Lisson Grove lingo; and I'm
not going to waste another cylinder on it. (*To the girl*) Be off
with you: I dont want you.

The Flower Girl. Dont you be so saucy. You aint heard what I
come for yet. (*To* MRS PEARCE, *who is waiting at the door for fur-*
ther instruction) Did you tell him I come in a taxi?

Mrs Pearce. Nonsense, girl! what do you think a gentleman
like Mr Higgins cares what you came in?

The Flower Girl. Oh, we are proud! He aint above giving
lessons, not him: I heard him say so. Well, I aint come here to
ask for any compliment; and if my money's not good enough
I can go elsewhere.

Higgins. Good enough for what?

The Flower Girl. Good enough for yə-oo. Now you know,
dont you? I'm coming to have lessons, I am. And to pay for
em tə-oo: make no mistake.

Higgins (*stupent*).[7] Well!!! (*Recovering his breath with a gasp*)
What do you expect me to say to you?

The Flower Girl. Well, if you was a gentleman, you might
ask me to sit down, I think. Dont I tell you I'm bringing you
business?

Higgins. Pickering: shall we ask this baggage to sit down, or
shall we throw her out of the window?

The Flower Girl (*running away in terror to the piano, where she*
turns at bay). Ah-ah-oh-ow-ow-ow-oo! (*Wounded and whimper-*
ing) I wont be called a baggage when Ive offered to pay like
any lady.

---

6. **feather-weight cross:** minor burden or inconvenience.
7. **stupent:** archaic word meaning "dumbfounded."

[*Motionless, the two men stare at her from the other side of the room, amazed.*]

Pickering (*gently*). But what is it you want?

The Flower Girl. I want to be a lady in a flower shop stead of sellin at the corner of Tottenham Court Road. But they wont take me unless I can talk more genteel. He said he could teach me. Well, here I am ready to pay him—not asking any favor—and he treats me zif I was dirt.

Mrs Pearce. How can you be such a foolish ignorant girl as to think you could afford to pay Mr Higgins?

The Flower Girl. Why shouldnt I? I know what lessons cost as well as you do; and I'm ready to pay.

Higgins. How much?

The Flower Girl (*coming back to him, triumphant*). Now youre talking! I thought youd come off it when you saw a chance of getting back a bit of what you chucked at me last night. (*Confidentially*) Youd had a drop in,[8] hadnt you?

Higgins (*peremptorily*). Sit down.

The Flower Girl. Oh, if youre going to make a compliment of it—

Higgins (*thundering at her*). Sit down.

Mrs Pearce (*severely*). Sit down, girl. Do as youre told.

The Flower Girl. Ah-ah-ah-ow-ow-oo! (*She stands, half rebellious, half bewildered*).

Pickering (*very courteous*). Wont you sit down? (*He places the stray chair near the hearthrug between himself and* HIGGINS).

Liza (*coyly*). Dont mind if I do. (*She sits down.* PICKERING *returns to the hearthrug*).

Higgins. Whats your name?

The Flower Girl. Liza Doolittle.

Higgins (*declaiming gravely*).

Eliza, Elizabeth, Betsy and Bess,
They went to the woods to get a bird's nes':

---

8. **had a drop in:** been drinking.

Pickering. They found a nest with four eggs in it:
Higgins. They took one apiece, and left three in it.

[*They laugh heartily at their own fun.*]

Liza. Oh, dont be silly.
Mrs Pearce (*placing herself behind* ELIZA's *chair*).You mustnt speak to the gentleman like that.
Liza. Well, why wont he speak sensible to me?
Higgins. Come back to business. How much do you propose to pay me for the lessons?
Liza. Oh, I know whats right. A lady friend of mine gets French lessons for eighteenpence an hour from a real French gentleman. Well, you wouldn't have the face to ask me the same for teaching me my own language as you would for French; so I wont give more than a shilling. Take it or leave it.
Higgins (*walking up and down the room, rattling his keys and his cash in his pockets*). You know, Pickering, if you consider a shilling, not as a simple shilling, but as a percentage of this girl's income, it works out as fully equivalent to sixty or seventy guineas from a millionaire.
Pickering. How so?
Higgins. Figure it out. A millionaire has about £150 a day. She earns about half-a-crown.
Liza (*haughtily*). Who told you I only—
Higgins (*continuing*). She offers me two-fifths of her day's income for a lesson. Two-fifths of a millionaire's income for a day would be somewhere about £60. It's handsome. By George, it's enormous! it's the biggest offer I ever had.
Liza (*rising, terrified*). Sixty pounds! What are you talking about? I never offered you sixty pounds. Where would I get—
Higgins. Hold your tongue.
Liza (*weeping*). But I aint got sixty pounds. Oh—
Mrs Pearce. Dont cry, you silly girl. Sit down. Nobody is going to touch your money.
Higgins. Somebody is going to touch you, with a broomstick, if you dont stop snivelling. Sit down.

Liza (*obeying slowly*). Ah-ah-ah-ow-oo-o! One would think you was my father.

Higgins. If I decide to teach you, I'll be worse than two fathers to you. Here! (*He offers her his silk handkerchief*).

Liza. Whats this for?

Higgins. To wipe your eyes. To wipe any part of your face that feels moist. Remember: thats your handkerchief; and thats your sleeve. Dont mistake the one for the other if you wish to become a lady in a shop.

[LIZA, *utterly bewildered, stares helplessly at him.*]

Mrs Pearce. It's no use talking to her like that, Mr Higgins: she doesnt understand you. Besides, youre quite wrong: she doesnt do it that way at all. (*She takes the handkerchief*).

Liza (*snatching it*). Here! You give me that handkerchief. He gev it to me, not to you.

Pickering (*laughing*). He did. I think it must be regarded as her property, Mrs Pearce.

Mrs Pearce (*resigning herself*). Serve you right, Mr Higgins.

Pickering. Higgins: I'm interested. What about the ambassador's garden party? I'll say youre the greatest teacher alive if you make that good. I'll bet you all the expenses of the experiment you cant do it. And I'll pay for the lessons.

Liza. Oh, you are real good. Thank you, Captain.

Higgins (*tempted, looking at her*). It's almost irresistible. She's so deliciously low—so horribly dirty—

Liza (*protesting extremely*). Ah-ah-ah-ah-ow-ow-oo-oo!!! I aint dirty: I washed my face and hands afore I come, I did.

Pickering. Youre certainly not going to turn her head with flattery, Higgins.

Mrs Pearce (*uneasy*). Oh, dont say that, sir: theres more ways than one of turning a girl's head; and nobody can do it better than Mr Higgins, though he may not always mean it. I do hope, sir, you wont encourage him to do anything foolish.

Higgins (*becoming excited as the idea grows on him*). What is life but a series of inspired follies? The difficulty is to find them to do. Never lose a chance: it doesnt come every day. I shall make a duchess of this draggletailed guttersnipe.

Liza (*strongly deprecating this view of her*). Ah-ah-ah-ow-ow-oo!

Higgins (*carried away*). Yes: in six months—in three if she has a good ear and a quick tongue—I'll take her anywhere and pass her off as anything. We'll start today: now! this moment! Take her away and clean her, Mrs Pearce. Monkey Brand, if it wont come off any other way. Is there a good fire in the kitchen?

Mrs Pearce (*protesting*). Yes; but—

Higgins (*storming on*). Take all her clothes off and burn them. Ring up Whiteley or somebody for new ones. Wrap her up in brown paper til they come.

Liza. Youre no gentleman, youre not, to talk of such things. I'm a good girl, I am; and I know what the like of you are, I do.

Higgins. We want none of your Lisson Grove prudery here, young woman. Youve got to learn to behave like a duchess. Take her away, Mrs Pearce. If she gives you any trouble, wallop her.

Liza (*springing up and running between* PICKERING *and* MRS PEARCE *for protection*). No! I'll call the police, I will.

Mrs Pearce. But Ive no place to put her.

Higgins. Put her in the dustbin.

Liza. Ah-ah-ah-ow-ow-oo!

Pickering. Oh come, Higgins! be reasonable.

Mrs Pearce (*resolutely*). You must be reasonable, Mr Higgins: really you must. You cant walk over everybody like this.

[HIGGINS, *thus scolded, subsides. The hurricane is succeeded by a zephyr of amiable surprise.*]

Higgins (*with professional exquisiteness of modulation*). I walk over everybody! My dear Mrs Pearce, my dear Pickering, I never had the slightest intention of walking over anyone. All I propose is that we should be kind to this poor girl. We must help her to prepare and fit herself for her new station in life. If

I did not express myself clearly it was because I did not wish to hurt her delicacy, or yours.

[LIZA, *reassured, steals back to her chair.*]

Mrs Pearce (*to* PICKERING). Well, did you ever hear anything like that, sir?

Pickering (*laughing heartily*). Never, Mrs Pearce: never.

Higgins (*patiently*). Whats the matter?

Mrs Pearce. Well, the matter is, sir, that you cant take a girl up like that as if you were picking up a pebble on the beach.

Higgins. Why not?

Mrs Pearce. Why not! But you dont know anything about her. What about her parents? She may be married.

Liza. Garn!

Higgins. There! As the girl very properly says, Garn! Married indeed! Dont you know that a woman of that class looks a worn out drudge of fifty a year after she's married?

Liza. Whood marry me?

Higgins (*suddenly resorting to the most thrillingly beautiful low tones in his best elocutionary style*). By George, Eliza, the streets will be strewn with the bodies of men shooting themselves for your sake before Ive done with you.

Mrs Pearce. Nonsense, sir. You mustnt talk like that to her.

Liza (*rising and squaring herself determinedly*). I'm going away. He's off his chump, he is. I dont want no balmies teaching me.

Higgins (*wounded in his tenderest point by her insensibility to his elocution*). Oh, indeed! I'm mad, am I? Very well, Mrs Pearce: you neednt order the new clothes for her. Throw her out.

Liza (*whimpering*). Nah-ow. You got no right to touch me.

Mrs Pearce. You see now what comes of being saucy. (*Indicating the door*) This way, please.

Liza (*almost in tears*). I didnt want no clothes. I wouldnt have taken them. (*She throws away the handkerchief*). I can buy my own clothes.

Higgins (*deftly retrieving the handkerchief and intercepting her on her reluctant way to the door*). Youre an ungrateful wicked girl.

This is my return for offering to take you out of the gutter and dress you beautifully and make a lady of you.

Mrs Pearce. Stop, Mr Higgins. I wont allow it. It's you that are wicked. Go home to your parents, girl; and tell them to take better care of you.

Liza. I aint got no parents. They told me I was big enough to earn my own living and turned me out.

Mrs Pearce. Wheres your mother?

Liza. I aint got no mother. Her that turned me out was my sixth stepmother. But I done without them. And I'm a good girl, I am.

Higgins. Very well, then, what on earth is all this fuss about? The girl doesnt belong to anybody—is no use to anybody but me. (*He goes to* MRS PEARCE *and begins coaxing*). You can adopt her, Mrs Pearce: I'm sure a daughter would be a great amusement to you. Now dont make any more fuss. Take her downstairs; and—

Mrs Pearce. But whats to become of her? Is she to be paid anything? Do be sensible, sir.

Higgins. Oh, pay her whatever is necessary: put it down in the housekeeping book. (*Impatiently*) What on earth will she want with money? She'll have her food and her clothes. She'll only drink if you give her money.

Liza (*turning on him*). Oh you are a brute. It's a lie: nobody ever saw the sign of liquor on me. (*To* PICKERING) Oh, sir: youre a gentleman: dont let him speak to me like that.

Pickering (*in good-humored remonstrance*). Does it occur to you, Higgins, that the girl has some feelings?

Higgins (*looking critically at her*). Oh no, I dont think so. Not any feelings that we need bother about. (*Cheerily*) Have you, Eliza?

Liza. I got my feelings same as anyone else.

Higgins (*to* PICKERING, *reflectively*). You see the difficulty?

Pickering. Eh? What difficulty?

Higgins. To get her to talk grammar. The mere pronunciation is easy enough.

Liza. I dont want to talk grammar. I want to talk like a lady in a flower shop.

Mrs Pearce. Will you please keep to the point, Mr Higgins. I want to know on what terms the girl is to be here. Is she to have any wages? And what is to become of her when youve finished your teaching? You must look ahead a little.

Higgins (*impatiently*). Whats to become of her if I leave her in the gutter? Tell me that, Mrs Pearce.

Mrs Pearce. Thats her own business, not yours, Mr Higgins.

Higgins. Well, when Ive done with her, we can throw her back into the gutter; and then it will be her own business again; so thats all right.

Liza. Oh, youve no feeling heart in you: you dont care for nothing but yourself. (*She rises and takes the floor resolutely*). Here! Ive had enough of this. I'm going (*making for the door*). You ought to be ashamed of yourself, you ought.

Higgins (*snatching a chocolate cream from the piano, his eyes suddenly beginning to twinkle with mischief*). Have some chocolates, Eliza.

Liza (*halting, tempted*). How do I know what might be in them? Ive heard of girls being drugged by the like of you.

[HIGGINS *whips out his penknife; cuts a chocolate in two; puts one half into his mouth and bolts it;*[9] *and offers her the other half.*]

Higgins. Pledge of good faith, Eliza. I eat one half: you eat the other. (LIZA *opens her mouth to retort: he pops the half chocolate into it*). You shall have boxes of them, barrels of them, every day. You shall live on them. Eh?

Liza (*who has disposed of the chocolate after being nearly choked by it*). I wouldnt have ate it, only I'm too ladylike to take it out of my mouth.

Higgins. Listen, Eliza. I think you said you came in a taxi.

Liza. Well, what if I did? Ive as good a right to take a taxi as anyone else.

Higgins. You have, Eliza; and in future you shall have as many taxis as you want. You shall go up and down and round the town in a taxi every day. Think of that, Eliza.

---

9. **bolts it:** chews and swallows it quickly.

Mrs Pearce. Mr Higgins: youre tempting the girl. It's not right. She should think of the future.

Higgins. At her age! Nonsense! Time enough to think of the future when you havnt any future to think of. No, Eliza: do as this lady does: think of other people's futures; but never think of your own. Think of chocolates, and taxis, and gold, and diamonds.

Liza. No: I dont want no gold and no diamonds. I'm a good girl, I am. (*She sits down again, with an attempt at dignity*).

Higgins. You shall remain so, Eliza, under the care of Mrs Pearce. And you shall marry an officer in the Guards, with a beautiful moustache: the son of a marquis, who will disinherit him for marrying you, but will relent when he sees your beauty and goodness—

Pickering. Excuse me, Higgins; but I really must interfere. Mrs Pearce is quite right. If this girl is to put herself in your hands for six months for an experiment in teaching, she must understand thoroughly what she's doing.

Higgins. How can she? She's incapable of understanding anything. Besides, do any of us understand what we are doing? If we did, would we ever do it?

Pickering. Very clever, Higgins; but not to the present point. (*To* ELIZA) Miss Doolittle—

Liza (*overwhelmed*). Ah-ah-ow-oo!

Higgins. There! Thats all youll get out of Eliza. Ah-ah-ow-oo! No use explaining. As a military man you ought to know that. Give her her orders: thats enough for her. Eliza: you are to live here for the next six months, learning how to speak beautifully, like a lady in a florist's shop. If youre good and do whatever youre told, you shall sleep in a proper bedroom, and have lots to eat, and money to buy chocolates and take rides in taxis. If youre naughty and idle you will sleep in the back kitchen among the black beetles, and be walloped by Mrs Pearce with a broomstick. At the end of six months you shall go to Buckingham Palace in a carriage, beautifully dressed. If the King finds out youre not a lady, you will be taken by the police to the Tower of London, where your head will be cut off as a warning to other presumptuous flower girls. If you are not found out, you shall have a present of seven-and-sixpence to start life with as a lady in a shop. If you refuse this offer you will be a most ungrateful wicked girl; and the angels will weep for you. (*To* PICKERING) Now are you satisfied, Pickering? (*To* MRS PEARCE) Can I put it more plainly and fairly, Mrs Pearce?

Mrs Pearce (*patiently*). I think youd better let me speak to the girl properly in private. I dont know that I can take charge of her or consent to the arrangement at all. Of course I know you dont mean her any harm; but when you get what you call interested in people's accents, you never think or care what may happen to them or you. Come with me, Eliza.

Higgins. Thats all right. Thank you, Mrs Pearce. Bundle her off to the bath-room.

Liza (*rising reluctantly and suspiciously*). Youre a great bully, you are. I wont stay here if I dont like. I wont let nobody wallop me. I never asked to go to Bucknam Palace, I didnt. I was never in trouble with the police, not me. I'm a good girl—

Mrs Pearce. Dont answer back, girl. You dont understand the gentleman. Come with me. (*She leads the way to the door, and holds it open for* ELIZA).

Liza (*as she goes out*). Well, what I say is right. I wont go near the King, not if I'm going to have my head cut off. If I'd known what I was letting myself in for, I wouldnt have come here. I always been a good girl; and I never offered to say a word to him; and I dont owe him nothing; and I dont care; and I wont be put upon; and I have my feelings the same as anyone else—

[MRS PEARCE *shuts the door; and* ELIZA'*s plaints are no longer audible.*]

* * *

Eliza is taken upstairs to the third floor greatly to her surprise; for she expected to be taken down to the scullery. There Mrs Pearce opens a door and takes her into a spare bedroom.

Mrs Pearce. I will have to put you here. This will be your bedroom.

Liza. O-h, I couldn't sleep here, missus. It's too good for the likes of me. I should be afraid to touch anything. I aint a duchess yet, you know.

Mrs Pearce. You have got to make yourself as clean as the room: then you wont be afraid of it. And you must call me Mrs Pearce, not missus. (*She throws open the door of the dressingroom, now modernized as a bathroom*).

Liza. Gawd! whats this? Is this where you wash clothes? Funny sort of copper[10] I call it.

Mrs Pearce. It is not a copper. This is where we wash ourselves, Eliza, and where I am going to wash you.

Liza. You expect me to get into that and wet myself all over! Not me. I should catch my death. I knew a woman did it every Saturday night; and she died of it.

Mrs Pearce. Mr Higgins has the gentlemen's bathroom downstairs; and he has a bath every morning, in cold water.

Liza. Ugh! He's made of iron, that man.

Mrs Pearce. If you are to sit with him and the Colonel and be taught you will have to do the same. They wont like the smell of you if you dont. But you can have the water as hot as you like. There are two taps: hot and cold.

Liza (*weeping*). I couldn't. I dursnt. Its not natural: it would kill me. Ive never had a bath in my life: not what youd call a proper one.

Mrs Pearce. Well, don't you want to be clean and sweet and decent, like a lady? You know you cant be a nice girl inside if youre a dirty slut outside.

Liza. Boohoo!!!!

Mrs Pearce. Now stop crying and go back into your room and take off all your clothes. Then wrap yourself in this (*taking down a gown from its peg and handing it to her*) and come back to me. I will get the bath ready.

---

10. **copper:** large boiler used for washing clothes.

Liza (*all tears*). I cant. I wont. I'm not used to it. Ive never took off all my clothes before. It's not right: it's not decent.

Mrs Pearce. Nonsense, child. Dont you take off all your clothes every night when you go to bed?

Liza (*amazed*). No. Why should I? I should catch my death. Of course I take off my skirt.

Mrs Pearce. Do you mean that you sleep in the underclothes you wear in the daytime?

Liza. What else have I to sleep in?

Mrs Pearce. You will never do that again as long as you live here. I will get you a proper nightdress.

Liza. Do you mean change into cold things and lie awake shivering half the night? You want to kill me, you do.

Mrs Pearce. I want to change you from a frowzy slut to a clean respectable girl fit to sit with the gentlemen in the study. Are you going to trust me and do what I tell you or be thrown out and sent back to your flower basket?

Liza. But you dont know what the cold is to me. You dont know how I dread it.

Mrs Pearce. Your bed wont be cold here: I will put a hot water bottle in it. (*Pushing her into the bedroom*) Off with you and undress.

Liza. Oh, if only I'd a known what a dreadful thing it is to be clean I'd never have come. I didnt know when I was well off. I— (MRS PEARCE *pushes her through the door, but leaves it partly open lest her prisoner should take to flight*).

[MRS PEARCE *puts on a pair of white rubber sleeves, and fills the bath, mixing hot and cold, and testing the result with the bath thermometer. She perfumes it with a handful of bath salts and adds a palmful of mustard. She then takes a formidable looking long handled scrubbing brush and soaps it profusely with a ball of scented soap.*

ELIZA *comes back with nothing on but the bath gown huddled tightly round her, a piteous spectacle of abject terror.*]

Mrs Pearce. Now come along. Take that thing off.

Liza. Oh I couldnt, Mrs Pearce: I reely couldnt. I never done such a thing.

Mrs Pearce. Nonsense. Here: step in and tell me whether its hot enough for you.

Liza. Ah-oo! Ah-oo. It's too hot.

Mrs Pearce (*deftly snatching the gown away and throwing* ELIZA *down on her back*). It wont hurt you. (*She sets to work with the scrubbing brush*).

[ELIZA's *screams are heartrending.*]

* * *

Meanwhile the Colonel has been having it out with Higgins about Eliza. Pickering has come from the hearth to the chair and seated himself astride of it with his arms on the back to cross-examine him.

Pickering. Excuse the straight question, Higgins. Are you a man of good character where women are concerned?

Higgins (*moodily*). Have you ever met a man of good character where women are concerned?

Pickering. Yes: very frequently.

Higgins (*dogmatically, lifting himself on his hands to the level of the piano, and sitting on it with a bounce*). Well, I havnt. I find that the moment I let a woman make friends with me, she becomes jealous, exacting, suspicious, and a damned nuisance. I find that the moment I let myself make friends with a woman, I become selfish and tyrannical. Women upset everything. When you let them into your life, you find that the woman is driving at one thing and youre driving at another.

Pickering. At what, for example?

Higgins (*coming off the piano restlessly*). Oh, Lord knows! I suppose the woman wants to live her own life; and the man wants to live his; and each tries to drag the other on to the wrong track. One wants to go north and the other south; and the result is that both have to go east, though they both hate the east wind. (*He sits down on the bench at the keyboard*). So here I am, a confirmed old bachelor, and likely to remain so.

Pickering (*rising and standing over him gravely*). Come, Higgins! You know what I mean. If I'm to be in this business I shall feel responsible for that girl. I hope it's understood that no advantage is to be taken of her position.

Higgins. What! That thing! Sacred, I assure you. (*Rising to explain*) You see, she'll be a pupil; and teaching would be impossible unless pupils were sacred. Ive taught scores of American millionairesses how to speak English: the best looking women in the world. I'm seasoned. They might as well be blocks of wood. *I* might as well be a block of wood. It's—

[MRS PEARCE *opens the door. She has* ELIZA's *hat in her hand.* PICKERING *retires to the easy-chair at the hearth and sits down.*]

Higgins (*eagerly*). Well, Mrs Pearce: is it all right?

Mrs Pearce (*at the door*). I just wish to trouble you with a word, if I may, Mr Higgins.

Higgins. Yes, certainly. Come in. (*She comes forward*). Dont burn that, Mrs Pearce. I'll keep it as a curiosity. (*He takes the hat*).

Mrs Pearce. Handle it carefully, sir, please. I had to promise her not to burn it; but I had better put it in the oven for a while.

Higgins (*putting it down hastily on the piano*). Oh! thank you. Well, what have you to say to me?

Pickering. Am I in the way?

Mrs Pearce. Not at all, sir. Mr Higgins: will you please be very particular what you say before the girl?

Higgins (*sternly*). Of course. I'm always particular about what I say. Why do you say this to me?

Mrs Pearce (*unmoved*). No sir: youre not at all particular when youve mislaid anything or when you get a little impatient. Now it doesnt matter before me: I'm used to it. But you really must not swear before the girl.

Higgins (*indignantly*). I swear! (*Most emphatically*) I never swear. I detest the habit. What the devil do you mean?

Mrs Pearce (*stolidly*). Thats what I mean, sir. You swear a great deal too much. I dont mind your damning and blasting, and what the devil and where the devil and who the devil—

Higgins. Mrs Pearce: this language from your lips! Really!

Mrs Pearce (*not to be put off*). —but there is a certain word I must ask you not to use. The girl used it herself when she began to enjoy the bath. It begins with the same letter as bath.[11] She knows no better: she learnt it at her mother's knee. But she must not hear it from your lips.

Higgins (*loftily*). I cannot charge myself with having ever uttered it, Mrs Pearce. (*She looks at him steadfastly. He adds, hiding an uneasy conscience with a judicial air*) Except perhaps in a moment of extreme and justifiable excitement.

Mrs Pearce. Only this morning, sir, you applied it to your boots, to the butter, and to the brown bread.

Higgins. Oh, that! Mere alliteration, Mrs Pearce, natural to a poet.

Mrs Pearce. Well, sir, whatever you choose to call it, I beg you not to let the girl hear you repeat it.

Higgins. Oh, very well, very well. Is that all?

Mrs Pearce. No, sir. We shall have to be very particular with this girl as to personal cleanliness.

Higgins. Certainly. Quite right. Most important.

Mrs Pearce. I mean not to be slovenly about her dress or untidy in leaving things about.

Higgins (*going to her solemnly*). Just so. I intended to call your attention to that. (*He passes on to* PICKERING, *who is enjoying the conversation immensely*). It is these little things that matter, Pickering. Take care of the pence and the pounds will take care of themselves is as true of personal habits as of money. (*He comes to anchor on the hearthrug, with the air of a man in an unassailable position*).

Mrs Pearce. Yes, sir. Then might I ask you not to come down to breakfast in your dressing-gown, or at any rate not to use it as a napkin to the extent you do, sir. And if you would be so good as not to eat everything off the same plate, and to remember not to put the porridge saucepan out of your hand

---

11. Mrs. Pearce is referring to the British slang word *bloody*, considered vulgar.

on the clean tablecloth, it would be a better example to the girl. You know you nearly choked yourself with a fishbone in the jam only last week.

Higgins (*routed from the hearthrug and drifting back to the piano*). I may do these things sometimes in absence of mind; but surely I dont do them habitually. (*Angrily*) By the way: my dressing-gown smells most damnably of benzine.

Mrs Pearce. No doubt it does, Mr Higgins. But if you will wipe your fingers—

Higgins (*yelling*). Oh very well, very well: I'll wipe them in my hair in future.

Mrs Pearce. I hope youre not offended, Mr Higgins.

Higgins (*shocked at finding himself thought capable of an unamiable sentiment*). Not at all, not at all. Youre quite right, Mrs Pearce: I shall be particularly careful before the girl. Is that all?

Mrs Pearce. No, sir. Might she use some of those Japanese dresses you brought from abroad? I really cant put her back into her old things.

Higgins. Certainly. Anything you like. Is that all?

Mrs Pearce. Thank you, sir. Thats all. (*She goes out*).

Higgins. You know, Pickering, that woman has the most extraordinary ideas about me. Here I am, a shy, diffident sort of man. Ive never been able to feel really grown-up and tremendous, like other chaps. And yet she's firmly persuaded that I'm an arbitrary overbearing bossing kind of person. I cant account for it.

[MRS PEARCE *returns.*]

Mrs Pearce. If you please, sir, the trouble's beginning already. Theres a dustman[12] downstairs, Alfred Doolittle, wants to see you. He says you have his daughter here.

Pickering (*rising*). Phew! I say!

Higgins (*promptly*). Send the blackguard up.

Mrs Pearce. Oh, very well, sir. (*She goes out*).

---

12. **dustman:** British word for "garbage collector."

Pickering. He may not be a blackguard, Higgins.

Higgins. Nonsense. Of course he's a blackguard.

Pickering. Whether he is or not, I'm afraid we shall have some trouble with him.

Higgins (*confidently*). Oh no: I think not. If theres any trouble he shall have it with me, not I with him. And we are sure to get something interesting out of him.

Pickering. About the girl?

Higgins. No. I mean his dialect.

Pickering. Oh!

Mrs Pearce (*at the door*). Doolittle, sir. (*She admits* DOOLITTLE *and retires*).

[ALFRED DOOLITTLE *is an elderly but vigorous dustman, clad in the costume of his profession, including a hat with a back brim covering his neck and shoulders. He has well marked and rather interesting features, and seems equally free from fear and conscience. He has a remarkably expressive voice, the result of a habit of giving vent to his feelings without reserve. His present pose is that of wounded honor and stern resolution.*]

Doolittle (*at the door, uncertain which of the two gentlemen is his man*). Professor Iggins?

Higgins. Here. Good morning. Sit down.

Doolittle. Morning, Governor. (*He sits down magisterially*). I come about a very serious matter, Governor.

Higgins (*to* PICKERING). Brought up in Hounslow. Mother Welsh, I should think. (DOOLITTLE *opens his mouth, amazed.* HIGGINS *continues*). What do you want, Doolittle?

Doolittle (*menacingly*). I want my daughter: thats what I want. See?

Higgins. Of course you do. Youre her father, arnt you? You dont suppose anyone else wants her, do you? I'm glad to see you have some spark of family feeling left. She's upstairs. Take her away at once.

Doolittle (*rising, fearfully taken aback*). What!

Higgins. Take her away. Do you suppose I'm going to keep your daughter for you?

Doolittle (*remonstrating*). Now, now, look here, Governor. Is this reasonable? Is it fairity to take advantage of a man like this? The girl belongs to me. You got her. Where do I come in? (*He sits down again*).

Higgins. Your daughter had the audacity to come to my house and ask me to teach her how to speak properly so that she could get a place in a flower shop. This gentleman and my housekeeper have been here all the time. (*Bullying him*) How dare you come here and attempt to blackmail me? You sent her here on purpose.

Doolittle (*protesting*). No, Governor.

Higgins. You must have. How else could you possibly know that she is here?

Doolittle. Dont take a man up like that, Governor.

Higgins. The police shall take you up. This is a plant—a plot to extort money by threats. I shall telephone for the police. (*He goes resolutely to the telephone and opens the directory*).

Doolittle. Have I asked you for a brass farthing? I leave it to the gentleman here: have I said a word about money?

Higgins (*throwing the book aside and marching down on* Doolittle *with a poser*). What else did you come for?

Doolittle (*sweetly*). Well, what would a man come for? Be human, Governor.

Higgins (*disarmed*). Alfred: did you put her up to it?

Doolittle. So help me, Governor, I never did. I take my Bible oath I aint seen the girl these two months past.

Higgins. Then how did you know she was here?

Doolittle (*"most musical, most melancholy"*). I'll tell you, Governor, if youll only let me get a word in. I'm willing to tell you. I'm wanting to tell you. I'm waiting to tell you.

Higgins. Pickering: this chap has a certain natural gift of rhetoric. Observe the rhythm of his native woodnotes wild. "I'm willing to tell you: I'm wanting to tell you: I'm waiting to tell you." Sentimental rhetoric! thats the Welsh strain in him. It also accounts for his mendacity and dishonesty.

Pickering. Oh, please, Higgins: I'm west country myself. (*To* Doolittle) How did you know the girl was here if you didnt send her?

Doolittle. It was like this, Governor. The girl took a boy in the taxi to give him a jaunt. Son of her landlady, he is. He hung about on the chance of her giving him another ride home. Well, she sent him back for her luggage when she heard you was willing for her to stop here. I met the boy at the corner of Long Acre and Endell Street.

Higgins. Public house.[13] Yes?

Doolittle. The poor man's club, Governor: why shouldnt I?

Pickering. Do let him tell his story, Higgins.

Doolittle. He told me what was up. And I ask you, what was my feelings and my duty as a father? I says to the boy, "You bring me the luggage," I says—

Pickering. Why didnt you go for it yourself?

Doolittle. Landlady wouldnt have trusted me with it, Governor. She's that kind of woman: you know. I had to give the boy a penny afore he trusted me with it, the little swine. I brought it to her just to oblige you like, and make myself agreeable. Thats all.

Higgins. How much luggage?

Doolittle. Musical instrument, Governor. A few pictures, a trifle of jewelry, and a bird-cage. She said she didnt want no clothes. What was I to think from that, Governor? I ask you as a parent what was I to think?

Higgins. So you came to rescue her from worse than death, eh?

Doolittle (*appreciatively: relieved at being so well understood*). Just so, Governor. Thats right.

Pickering. But why did you bring her luggage if you intended to take her away?

Doolittle. Have I said a word about taking her away? Have I now?

Higgins (*determinedly*). Youre going to take her away, double quick. (*He crosses to the hearth and rings the bell*).

Doolittle (*rising*). No, Governor. Dont say that. I'm not the man to stand in my girl's light. Heres a career opening for her as you might say; and—

---

13. **public house:** British word for "bar" or "tavern."

[MRS PEARCE *opens the door and awaits orders.*]

Higgins. Mrs Pearce: this is Eliza's father. He has come to take her away. Give her to him. (*He goes back to the piano, with an air of washing his hands of the whole affair*).

Doolittle. No. This is a misunderstanding. Listen here—

Mrs Pearce. He cant take her away, Mr Higgins: how can he? You told me to burn her clothes.

Doolittle. Thats right. I cant carry the girl through the streets like a blooming monkey, can I? I put it to you.

Higgins. You have put it to me that you want your daughter. Take your daughter. If she has no clothes go out and buy her some.

Doolittle (*desperate*). Wheres the clothes she come in? Did I burn them or did your missus here?

Mrs Pearce. I am the housekeeper, if you please. I have sent for some clothes for the girl. When they come you can take her away. You can wait in the kitchen. This way, please.

[DOOLITTLE, *much troubled, accompanies her to the door; then hesitates; finally turns confidentially to* HIGGINS.]

Doolittle. Listen here, Governor. You and me is men of the world, aint we?

Higgins. Oh! Men of the world, are we? Youd better go, Mrs Pearce.

Mrs Pearce. I think so, indeed, sir. (*She goes, with dignity*).

Pickering. The floor is yours, Mr Doolittle.

Doolittle (*to* PICKERING). I thank you, Governor. (*To* HIGGINS, *who takes refuge on the piano bench, a little overwhelmed by the proximity of his visitor; for* DOOLITTLE *has a professional flavor of dust about him*) Well, the truth is, Ive taken a sort of fancy to you, Governor; and if you want the girl, I'm not so set on having her back home again but what I might be open to an arrangement. Regarded in the light of a young woman, she's a fine handsome girl. As a daughter she's not worth her keep; and so I tell you straight. All I ask is my rights as a father; and youre the last man alive to expect me to let her go for nothing;

for I can see youre one of the straight sort, Governor. Well, whats a five-pound note to you? and whats Eliza to me? (*He turns to his chair and sits down judicially*).

Pickering. I think you ought to know, Doolittle, that Mr Higgins's intentions are entirely honorable.

Doolittle. Course they are, Governor. If I thought they wasn't, I'd ask fifty.

Higgins (*revolted*). Do you mean to say that you would sell your daughter for £50?

Doolittle. Not in a general way I wouldnt; but to oblige a gentleman like you I'd do a good deal, I do assure you.

Pickering. Have you no morals, man?

Doolittle (*unabashed*). Cant afford them, Governor. Neither could you if you was as poor as me. Not that I mean any harm, you know. But if Liza is going to have a bit out of this, why not me too?

Higgins (*troubled*). I dont know what to do, Pickering. There can be no question that as a matter of morals it's a positive crime to give this chap a farthing. And yet I feel a sort of rough justice in his claim.

Doolittle. Thats it, Governor. Thats all I say. A father's heart, as it were.

Pickering. Well, I know the feeling; but really it seems hardly right—

Doolittle. Dont say that, Governor. Dont look at it that way. What am I, Governors both? I ask you, what am I? I'm one of the undeserving poor: thats what I am. Think of what that means to a man. It means that he's up agen middle class morality all the time. If theres anything going, and I put in for a bit of it, it's always the same story: "Youre undeserving; so you cant have it." But my needs is as great as the most deserving widow's that ever got money out of six different charities in one week for the death of the same husband. I dont need less than a deserving man: I need more. I dont eat less hearty than him; and I drink a lot more. I want a bit of amusement, cause I'm a thinking man. I want cheerfulness and a song and a band when I feel low. Well, they charge me just the same for everything as they charge the deserving. What is middle class morality? Just an excuse for never giving me anything. Therefore, I ask you, as two gentlemen, not to play that game on me. I'm playing straight with you. I aint pretending to be deserving. I'm undeserving; and I mean to go on being undeserving. I like it; and thats the truth. Will you take advantage of a man's nature to do him out of the price of his own daughter what he's brought up and fed and clothed by the sweat of his brow until she's growed big enough to be interesting to you two gentlemen? Is five pounds unreasonable? I put it to you; and I leave it to you.

Higgins (*rising, and going over to* PICKERING). Pickering: if we were to take this man in hand for three months, he could choose between a seat in the Cabinet and a popular pulpit in Wales.

Pickering. What do you say to that, Doolittle?

Doolittle. Not me, Governor, thank you kindly. Ive heard all the preachers and all the prime ministers—for I'm a thinking man and game for politics or religion or social reform same as all the other amusements—and I tell you it's a dog's life any way you look at it. Undeserving poverty is my line. Taking one station in society with another, it's—it's—well, it's the only one that has any ginger in it, to my taste.

Higgins. I suppose we must give him a fiver.

Pickering. He'll make a bad use of it, I'm afraid.

Doolittle. Not me, Governor, so help me I wont. Dont you be afraid that I'll save it and spare it and live idle on it. There wont be a penny of it left by Monday: I'll have to go to work same as if I'd never had it. It wont pauperize me, you bet. Just one good spree for myself and the missus, giving pleasure to ourselves and employment to others, and satisfaction to you to think it's not been throwed away. You couldnt spend it better.

Higgins (*taking out his pocket book and coming between* DOOLITTLE *and the piano*). This is irresistible. Lets give him ten. (*He offers two notes to the dustman*).

Doolittle. No, Governor. She wouldnt have the heart to spend ten; and perhaps I shouldnt neither. Ten pounds is a lot of money: it makes a man feel prudent like; and then goodbye to happiness. You give me what I ask you, Governor: not a penny more, and not a penny less.

Pickering. Why dont you marry that missus of yours? I rather draw the line at encouraging that sort of immorality.

Doolittle. Tell her so, Governor: tell her so. I'm willing. It's me that suffers by it. Ive no hold on her. I got to be agreeable to her. I got to give her presents. I got to buy her clothes something sinful. I'm a slave to that woman, Governor, just because I'm not her lawful husband. And she knows it too. Catch her marrying me! Take my advice, Governor: marry Eliza while she's young and dont know no better. If you dont youll be sorry for it after. If you do, she'll be sorry for it after; but better her than you, because youre a man, and she's only a woman and dont know how to be happy anyhow.

Higgins. Pickering: If we listen to this man another minute, we shall have no convictions left. (*To* DOOLITTLE) Five pounds I think you said.

Doolittle. Thank you kindly, Governor.

Higgins. Youre sure you wont take ten?

Doolittle. Not now. Another time, Governor.

Higgins (*handing him a five-pound note*). Here you are.

Doolittle. Thank you, Governor. Good morning. (*He hurries to the door, anxious to get away with his booty. When he opens it he is confronted with a dainty and exquisitely clean young Japanese lady in a simple blue cotton kimono printed cunningly with small white jasmine blossoms.* MRS PEARCE *is with her. He gets out of her way deferentially and apologizes*). Beg pardon, miss.

The Japanese Lady. Garn! Dont you know your own daughter?

Doolittle.		
Higgins.	[*exclaiming simultaneously*]	Bly me! it's Eliza! Whats that? This!
Pickering.		By Jove!

Liza. Dont I look silly?

Higgins. Silly?

Mrs Pearce (*at the door*). Now, Mr Higgins, please dont say anything to make the girl conceited about herself.

Higgins (*conscientiously*). Oh! Quite right, Mrs Pearce. (*To* ELIZA) Yes: damned silly.

Mrs Pearce. Please, sir.

Higgins (*correcting himself*). I mean extremely silly.

Liza. I should look all right with my hat on. (*She takes up her hat; puts it on; and walks across the room to the fireplace with a fashionable air*).

Higgins. A new fashion, by George! And it ought to look horrible!

Doolittle (*with fatherly pride*). Well, I never thought she'd clean up as good looking as that, Governor. She's a credit to me, aint she?

Liza. I tell you, it's easy to clean up here. Hot and cold water on tap, just as much as you like, there is. Woolly towels, there is; and a towel horse[14] so hot, it burns your fingers. Soft brushes to scrub yourself, and a wooden bowl of soap smelling like primroses. Now I know why ladies is so clean. Washing's a treat for them. Wish they could see what it is for the like of me!

Higgins. I'm glad the bathroom met with your approval.

Liza. It didnt: not all of it; and I dont care who hears me say it. Mrs Pearce knows.

Higgins. What was wrong, Mrs Pearce?

Mrs Pearce (*blandly*). Oh, nothing, sir. It doesnt matter.

Liza. I had a good mind to break it. I didnt know which way to look. But I hung a towel over it, I did.

Higgins. Over what?

Mrs Pearce. Over the looking-glass, sir.

Higgins. Doolittle: you have brought your daughter up too strictly.

Doolittle. Me! I never brought her up at all, except to give her a lick of a strap now and again. Dont put it on me, Governor. She aint accustomed to it, you see: thats all. But she'll soon pick up your free-and-easy ways.

Liza. I'm a good girl, I am; and I wont pick up no free-and-easy ways.

---

14. **towel horse:** towel rack; here, one with a built-in heater for drying towels.

Higgins. Eliza: if you say again that youre a good girl, your father shall take you home.

Liza. Not him. You dont know my father. All he come here for was to touch you for some money to get drunk on.

Doolittle. Well, what else would I want money for? To put into the plate in church, I suppose. (*She puts out her tongue at him. He is so incensed by this that* PICKERING *presently finds it necessary to step between them*). Dont you give me none of your lip; and dont let me hear you giving this gentleman any of it neither, or youll hear from me about it. See?

Higgins. Have you any further advice to give her before you go, Doolittle? Your blessing, for instance.

Doolittle. No, Governor: I aint such a mug as to put up my children to all I know myself. Hard enough to hold them in without that. If you want Eliza's mind improved, Governor, you do it yourself with a strap. So long, gentlemen. (*He turns to go*).

Higgins (*impressively*). Stop. Youll come regularly to see your daughter. It's your duty, you know. My brother is a clergyman; and he could help you in your talks with her.

Doolittle (*evasively*). Certainly, I'll come, Governor. Not just this week, because I have a job at a distance. But later on you may depend on me. Afternoon, gentlemen. Afternoon, maam. (*He touches his hat to* MRS PEARCE, *who disdains the salutation and goes out. He winks at* HIGGINS, *thinking him probably a fellow-sufferer from* MRS PEARCE's *difficult disposition, and follows her*).

Liza. Dont you believe the old liar. He'd as soon you set a bulldog on him as a clergyman. You wont see him again in a hurry.

Higgins. I dont want to, Eliza. Do you?

Liza. Not me. I dont want never to see him again, I dont. He's a disgrace to me, he is, collecting dust, instead of working at his trade.

Pickering. What is his trade, Eliza?

Liza. Talking money out of other people's pockets into his own. His proper trade's a navvy;[15] and he works at it some-

---

15. **navvy** (nav´ē): British word for "unskilled laborer."

times too—for exercise—and earns good money at it. Aint you going to call me Miss Doolittle any more?

Pickering. I beg your pardon, Miss Doolittle. It was a slip of the tongue.

Liza. Oh, I dont mind; only it sounded so genteel. I should just like to take a taxi to the corner of Tottenham Court Road and get out there and tell it to wait for me, just to put the girls in their place a bit. I wouldnt speak to them, you know.

Pickering. Better wait til we get you something really fashionable.

Higgins. Besides, you shouldnt cut your old friends now that you have risen in the world. Thats what we call snobbery.

Liza. You dont call the like of them my friends now, I should hope. Theyve took it out of me often enough with their ridicule when they had the chance; and now I mean to get a bit of my own back. But if I'm to have fashionable clothes, I'll wait. I should like to have some. Mrs Pearce says youre going to give me some to wear to bed at night different to what I wear in the daytime; but it do seem a waste of money when you could get something to shew. Besides, I never could fancy changing into cold things on a winter night.

Mrs Pearce (*coming back*). Now, Eliza. The new things have come for you to try on.

Liza. Ah-ow-oo-ooh! (*She rushes out*).

Mrs Pearce (*following her*). Oh, dont rush about like that, girl. (*She shuts the door behind her*).

Higgins. Pickering: we have taken on a stiff job.

Pickering (*with conviction*). Higgins: we have.

* * *

There seems to be more curiosity as to what Higgins's lessons to Eliza were like. Well, here is a sample: the first one.

Picture Eliza, in her new clothes, and feeling her inside put out of step by a lunch, dinner, and breakfast of a kind to which it is unaccustomed, seated with Higgins and the Colonel in the study, feeling like a hospital out-patient at a first encounter with the doctors.

Higgins, constitutionally unable to sit still, discomposes her still more by striding restlessly about. But for the reassuring presence and quietude of her friend the Colonel she would run for her life, even back to Drury Lane.

Higgins. Say your alphabet.

Liza. I know my alphabet. Do you think I know nothing? I dont need to be taught like a child.

Higgins (*thundering*). Say your alphabet.

Pickering. Say it, Miss Doolittle. You will understand presently. Do what he tells you; and let him teach you in his own way.

Liza. Oh well, if you put it like that—Ahyee, bəyee, cəyee, dəyee—

Higgins (*with the roar of a wounded lion*). Stop. Listen to this, Pickering. This is what we pay for as elementary education. This unfortunate animal has been locked up for nine years in school at our expense to teach her to speak and read the language of Shakespear and Milton. And the result is Ahyee, Bə-yee, Cə-yee, Də-yee. (*To* ELIZA) Say A, B, C, D.

Liza (*almost in tears*). But I'm saying it. Ahyee, Bəee, Cə-ee—

Higgins. Stop. Say a cup of tea.

Liza. A cappətə-ee.

Higgins. Put your tongue forward until it squeezes against the top of your lower teeth. Now say cup.

Liza. C-c-c—I cant. C-cup.

Pickering. Good. Splendid, Miss Doolittle.

Higgins. By Jupiter, she's done it at the first shot. Pickering: we shall make a duchess of her. (*To* ELIZA) Do you think you could possible say tea? Not tə-yee, mind: if you ever say bə-yee, cə-yee, də-yee again you shall be dragged round the room three times by the hair of your head. (*Fortissimo*)[16] T, T, T, T.

---

16. *fortissimo* (fôr·tis′ə·mō′): Italian for "very loud"; a term used as a direction in music.

Liza (*weeping*). I cant hear no difference cep that it sounds more genteel-like when you say it.

Higgins. Well, if you can hear that difference, what the devil are you crying for? Pickering: give her a chocolate.

Pickering. No, no. Never mind crying a little, Miss Doolittle: you are doing very well; and the lessons wont hurt. I promise you I wont let him drag you round the room by your hair.

Higgins. Be off with you to Mrs Pearce and tell her about it. Think about it. Try to do it by yourself: and keep your tongue well forward in your mouth instead of trying to roll it up and swallow it. Another lesson at half-past four this afternoon. Away with you.

[ELIZA, *still sobbing, rushes from the room.*]

And that is the sort of ordeal poor Eliza has to go through for months before we meet her again on her first appearance in London society of the professional class.

Act III

It is MRS HIGGINS's *at-home day.*[1] *Nobody has yet arrived. Her drawing room, in a flat on Chelsea Embankment, has three windows looking on the river; and the ceiling is not so lofty as it would be in an older house of the same pretension. The windows are open, giving access to a balcony with flowers in pots. If you stand with your face to the windows, you have the fireplace on your left and the door in the right-hand wall close to the corner nearest the windows.*

MRS HIGGINS *was brought up on Morris and Burne Jones;*[2] *and her room, which is very unlike her son's room in Wimpole Street, is not crowded with furniture and little tables and nicknacks. In the middle of the room there is a big ottoman; and this, with the carpet, the Morris wall-papers, and the Morris chintz window curtains and brocade covers of the ottoman and its cushions, supply all the ornament, and are much too handsome to be hidden by odds and ends of useless things. A few good oil-paintings from the exhibitions in the Grosvenor Gallery thirty years ago (the Burne Jones, not the Whistler*[3] *side of them) are on the walls. The only landscape is a Cecil Lawson*[4] *on the scale of a Rubens.*[5] *There is a portrait of* MRS HIGGINS *as she was when she defied the fashion in her youth in*

---

1. **at-home day:** day on which a lady receives visitors who do not have specific invitations.
2. **Morris and Burne Jones:** William Morris (1834–1896) and Sir Edward Coley Burne-Jones (1833–1898) were English artists who influenced interior design in Victorian England.
3. **Whistler:** James Abbott McNeill Whistler (1834–1903), an American painter who spent many years in England.
4. **Cecil Lawson:** Cecil Gordon Lawson (1851–1882), an English landscape painter.
5. **Rubens:** painting by Peter Paul Rubens (1577–1640), a Flemish artist known for his large paintings.

one of the beautiful Rossettian[6] costumes which, when caricatured by people who did not understand, led to the absurdities of popular estheticism in the eighteen-seventies.

In the corner diagonally opposite the door MRS HIGGINS, now over sixty and long past taking the trouble to dress out of the fashion, sits writing at an elegantly simple writing-table with a bell button within reach of her hand. There is a Chippendale chair further back in the room between her and the window nearest her side. At the other side of the room, further forward, is an Elizabethan chair roughly carved in the taste of Inigo Jones. On the same side a piano in a decorated case. The corner between the fireplace and the window is occupied by a divan cushioned in Morris chintz.

It is between four and five in the afternoon.

The door is opened violently; and HIGGINS enters with his hat on.

Mrs Higgins (*dismayed*). Henry! (*Scolding him*) What are you doing here today? It is my at-home day: you promised not to come. (*As he bends to kiss her, she takes his hat off, and presents it to him*).

Higgins. Oh bother! (*He throws the hat down on the table*).

Mrs Higgins. Go home at once.

Higgins (*kissing her*). I know, mother. I came on purpose.

Mrs Higgins. But you mustnt. I'm serious, Henry. You offend all my friends: they stop coming whenever they meet you.

Higgins. Nonsense! I know I have no small talk; but people dont mind. (*He sits on the settee*).

Mrs Higgins. Oh! dont they? Small talk indeed! What about your large talk? Really, dear, you mustnt stay.

Higgins. I must. Ive a job for you. A phonetic job.

Mrs Higgins. No use, dear. I'm sorry; but I cant get round your vowels; and though I like to get pretty postcards in your patent shorthand, I always have to read the copies in ordinary writing you so thoughtfully send me.

---

6. **Rossettian:** of a style associated with the paintings of the English artist Dante Gabriel Rossetti (rə·zet´ē) (1828–1882).

Higgins. Well, this isnt a phonetic job.

Mrs Higgins. You said it was.

Higgins. Not your part of it. Ive picked up a girl.

Mrs Higgins. Does that mean that some girl has picked you up?

Higgins. Not at all. I dont mean a love affair.

Mrs Higgins. What a pity!

Higgins. Why?

Mrs Higgins. Well, you never fall in love with anyone under forty-five. When will you discover that there are some rather nice-looking young women about?

Higgins. Oh, I cant be bothered with young women. My idea of a lovable woman is somebody as like you as possible. I shall never get into the way of seriously liking young women: some habits lie too deep to be changed. (*Rising abruptly and walking about, jingling his money and his keys in his trouser pockets*) Besides, theyre all idiots.

Mrs Higgins. Do you know what you would do if you really loved me, Henry?

Higgins. Oh bother! What? Marry, I suppose?

Mrs Higgins. No. Stop fidgeting and take your hands out of your pockets. (*With a gesture of despair, he obeys and sits down again*). Thats a good boy. Now tell me about the girl.

Higgins. She's coming to see you.

Mrs Higgins. I dont remember asking her.

Higgins. You didnt. *I* asked her. If youd known her you wouldnt have asked her.

Mrs Higgins. Indeed! Why?

Higgins. Well, it's like this. She's a common flower girl. I picked her off the kerbstone.

Mrs Higgins. And invited her to my at-home!

Higgins (*rising and coming to her to coax her*). Oh, thatll be all right. Ive taught her to speak properly; and she has strict orders as to her behavior. She's to keep to two subjects: the weather and everybody's health—Fine day and How do you do, you know—and not to let herself go on things in general. That will be safe.

Mrs Higgins. Safe! To talk about our health! about our insides! perhaps about our outsides! How could you be so silly, Henry?

Higgins (*impatiently*). Well, she must talk about something. (*He controls himself and sits down again*). Oh, she'll be all right: dont you fuss. Pickering is in it with me. Ive a sort of bet on that I'll pass her off as a duchess in six months. I started on her some months ago; and she's getting on like a house on fire. I shall win my bet. She has a quick ear; and she's been easier to teach than my middle-class pupils because she's had to learn a complete new language. She talks English almost as you talk French.

Mrs Higgins. Thats satisfactory, at all events.

Higgins. Well, it is and it isnt.

Mrs Higgins. What does that mean?

Higgins. You see, Ive got her pronunciation all right; but you have to consider not only how a girl pronounces, but what she pronounces; and thats where—

[*They are interrupted by the parlormaid, announcing guests.*]

The Parlormaid. Mrs and Miss Eynsford Hill. (*She withdraws*).

Higgins. Oh Lord! (*He rises; snatches his hat from the table; and makes for the door; but before he reaches it his mother introduces him*).

[MRS *and* MISS EYNSFORD HILL *are the mother and daughter who sheltered from the rain in Covent Garden. The mother is well bred, quiet, and has the habitual anxiety of straitened means. The daughter has acquired a gay air of being very much at home in society: the bravado of genteel poverty.*]

Mrs Eynsford Hill (*to* MRS HIGGINS). How do you do? (*They shake hands*).

Miss Eynsford Hill. How d'you do? (*She shakes*).

Mrs Higgins (*introducing*). My son Henry.

Mrs Eynsford Hill. Your celebrated son! I have so longed to meet you, Professor Higgins.

Higgins (*glumly, making no movement in her direction*). Delighted. (*He backs against the piano and bows brusquely*).

Miss Eynsford Hill (*going to him with confident familiarity*). How do you do?

Higgins (*staring at her*). Ive seen you before somewhere. I havent the ghost of a notion where; but Ive heard your voice. (*Drearily*) It doesnt matter. Youd better sit down.

Mrs Higgins. I'm sorry to say that my celebrated son has no manners. You mustnt mind him.

Miss Eynsford Hill (*gaily*). I dont. (*She sits in the Elizabethan chair*).

Mrs Eynsford Hill (*a little bewildered*). Not at all. (*She sits on the ottoman between her daughter and* MRS HIGGINS, *who has turned her chair away from the writing-table*).

Higgins. Oh, have I been rude? I didnt mean to be.

[*He goes to the central window, through which, with his back to the company, he contemplates the river and the flowers in Battersea Park on the opposite bank as if they were a frozen desert.*

The parlormaid returns, ushering in PICKERING.]

The Parlormaid. Colonel Pickering. (*She withdraws*).

Pickering. How do you do, Mrs Higgins?

Mrs Higgins. So glad youve come. Do you know Mrs Eynsford Hill—Miss Eynsford Hill? (*Exchange of bows. The Colonel brings the Chippendale chair a little forward between* MRS HILL *and* MRS HIGGINS, *and sits down*).

Pickering. Has Henry told you what weve come for?

Higgins (*over his shoulder*). We were interrupted: damn it!

Mrs Higgins. Oh Henry, Henry, really!

Mrs Eynsford Hill (*half rising*). Are we in the way?

Mrs Higgins (*rising and making her sit down again*). No, no. You couldnt have come more fortunately: we want you to meet a friend of ours.

Higgins (*turning hopefully*). Yes, by George! We want two or three people. Youll do as well as anybody else.

[*The parlormaid returns, ushering* FREDDY.]

The Parlormaid. Mr Eynsford Hill.

Higgins (*almost audibly, past endurance*). God of Heaven! another of them.

Freddy (*shaking hands with* MRS HIGGINS). Ahdedo?

Mrs Higgins. Very good of you to come. (*Introducing*) Colonel Pickering.

Freddy (*bowing*). Ahdedo?

Mrs Higgins. I dont think you know my son, Professor Higgins.

Freddy (*going to* HIGGINS). Ahdedo?

Higgins (*looking at him much as if he were a pickpocket*). I'll take my oath Ive met you before somewhere. Where was it?

Freddy. I dont think so.

Higgins (*resignedly*). It dont matter, anyhow. Sit down.

[*He shakes* FREDDY's *hand, and almost slings him on to the ottoman with his face to the windows; then comes round to the other side of it.*]

Higgins. Well, here we are, anyhow! (*He sits down on the ottoman next* MRS EYNSFORD HILL, *on her left*). And now, what the devil are we going to talk about until Eliza comes?

Mrs Higgins. Henry: you are the life and soul of the Royal Society's soirées;[7] but really youre rather trying on more commonplace occasions.

Higgins. Am I? Very sorry. (*Beaming suddenly*) I suppose I am, you know. (*Uproariously*) Ha, ha!

Miss Eynsford Hill (*who considers* HIGGINS *quite eligible matrimonially*). I sympathize. *I* havnt any small talk. If people would only be frank and say what they really think!

Higgins (*relapsing into gloom*). Lord forbid!

Mrs Eynsford Hill (*taking up her daughter's cue*). But why?

---

7. **soirées** (swä·räz´): parties held in the evening.

Higgins. What they think they ought to think is bad enough, Lord knows; but what they really think would break up the whole show. Do you suppose it would be really agreeable if I were to come out now with what *I* really think?

Miss Eynsford Hill (*gaily*). Is it so very cynical?

Higgins. Cynical! Who the dickens said it was cynical? I mean it wouldnt be decent.

Mrs Eynsford Hill (*seriously*). Oh! I'm sure you dont mean that, Mr Higgins.

Higgins. You see, we're all savages, more or less. We're supposed to be civilized and cultured—to know all about poetry and philosophy and art and science, and so on; but how many of us know even the meanings of these names? (*To* MISS HILL) What do you know of poetry? (*To* MRS HILL) What do you know of science? (*Indicating* FREDDY) What does he know of art or science or anything else? What the devil do you imagine I know of philosophy?

Mrs Higgins (*warningly*). Or of manners, Henry?

The Parlormaid (*opening the door*). Miss Doolittle. (*She withdraws*).

Higgins (*rising hastily and running to* MRS HIGGINS). Here she is, mother. (*He stands on tiptoe and makes signs over his mother's head to* ELIZA *to indicate to her which lady is her hostess*).

[ELIZA, *who is exquisitely dressed, produces an impression of such remarkable distinction and beauty as she enters that they all rise, quite fluttered. Guided by* HIGGINS's *signals, she comes to* MRS HIGGINS *with studied grace.*]

Liza (*speaking with pedantic correctness of pronunciation and great beauty of tone*). How do you do, Mrs Higgins? (*She gasps slightly in making sure of the H in Higgins, but is quite successful*). Mr Higgins told me I might come.

Mrs Higgins (*cordially*). Quite right: I'm very glad indeed to see you.

Pickering. How do you do, Miss Doolittle?

Liza (*shaking hands with him*). Colonel Pickering, is it not?

Mrs Eynsford Hill. I feel sure we have met before, Miss Doolittle. I remember your eyes.

Liza. How do you do? (*She sits down on the ottoman gracefully in the place just left vacant by* HIGGINS).

Mrs Eynsford Hill (*introducing*). My daughter Clara.

Liza. How do you do?

Clara (*impulsively*). How do you do? (*She sits down on the ottoman beside* ELIZA, *devouring her with her eyes*).

Freddy (*coming to their side of the ottoman*). Ive certainly had the pleasure.

Mrs Eynsford Hill (*introducing*). My son Freddy.

Liza. How do you do?

[FREDDY *bows and sits down in the Elizabethan chair, infatuated.*]

Higgins (*suddenly*). By George, yes: it all comes back to me! (*They stare at him*). Covent Garden! (*Lamentably*) What a damned thing!

Mrs Higgins. Henry, please! (*He is about to sit on the edge of the table*). Dont sit on my writing-table: youll break it.

Higgins (*sulkily*). Sorry.

[*He goes to the divan, stumbling into the fender and over the fire-irons on his way; extricating himself with muttered imprecations; and finishing his disastrous journey by throwing himself so impatiently on the divan that he almost breaks it.* MRS HIGGINS *looks at him, but controls herself and says nothing.*

A long and painful pause ensues.]

Mrs Higgins (*at last, conversationally*). Will it rain, do you think?

Liza. The shallow depression in the west of these islands is likely to move slowly in an easterly direction. There are no indications of any great change in the barometrical situation.

Freddy. Ha! ha! how awfully funny!

Liza. What is wrong with that, young man? I bet I got it right.

Freddy. Killing!

Mrs Eynsford Hill. I'm sure I hope it wont turn cold. Theres so much influenza about. It runs right through our whole family regularly every spring.

Liza (*darkly*). My aunt died of influenza: so they said.

Mrs Eynsford Hill (*clicks her tongue sympathetically*)!!!

Liza (*in the same tragic tone*). But it's my belief they done the old woman in.

Mrs Higgins (*puzzled*). Done her in?

Liza. Y-e-e-e-es, Lord love you! Why should she die of influenza? She come through diphtheria right enough the year before. I saw her with my own eyes. Fairly blue with it, she was. They all thought she was dead; but my father he kept ladling gin down her throat til she came to so sudden that she bit the bowl off the spoon.

Mrs Eynsford Hill (*startled*). Dear me!

Liza (*piling up the indictment*). What call would a woman with that strength in her have to die of influenza? What become of her new straw hat that should have come to me? Somebody pinched it; and what I say is, them as pinched it done her in.

Mrs Eynsford Hill. What does doing her in mean?

Higgins (*hastily*). Oh, thats the new small talk. To do a person in means to kill them.

Mrs Eynsford Hill (*to* ELIZA, *horrified*). You surely dont believe that your aunt was killed?

Liza. Do I not! Them she lived with would have killed her for a hat-pin, let alone a hat.

Mrs Eynsford Hill. But it cant have been right for your father to pour spirits down her throat like that. It might have killed her.

Liza. Not her. Gin was mother's milk to her. Besides, he'd poured so much down his own throat that he knew the good of it.

Mrs Eynsford Hill. Do you mean that he drank?

Liza. Drank! My word! Something chronic.

Mrs Eynsford Hill. How dreadful for you!

Liza. Not a bit. It never did him no harm what I could see. But then he did not keep it up regular. (*Cheerfully*) On the burst, as you might say, from time to time. And always more agreeable when he had a drop in. When he was out of work, my mother used to give him fourpence and tell him to go out and not come back until he'd drunk himself cheerful and loving-like. Theres lots of women has to make their husbands drunk to make them fit to live with. (*Now quite at her ease*) You see, it's like this. If a man has a bit of a conscience, it always takes him when he's sober; and then it makes him low-spirited. A drop of booze just takes that off and makes him happy. (*To* FREDDY, *who is in convulsions of suppressed laughter*) Here! what are you sniggering at?

Freddy. The new small talk. You do it so awfully well.

Liza. If I was doing it proper, what was you laughing at? (*To* HIGGINS) Have I said anything I oughtnt?

Mrs Higgins (*interposing*). Not at all, Miss Doolittle.

Liza. Well, thats a mercy, anyhow. (*Expansively*) What I always say is—

Higgins (*rising and looking at his watch*). Ahem!

Liza (*looking round at him; taking the hint; and rising*). Well: I must go. (*They all rise.* FREDDY *goes to the door*). So pleased to have met you. Goodbye. (*She shakes hands with* MRS HIGGINS).

Mrs Higgins. Goodbye.

Liza. Goodbye, Colonel Pickering.

Pickering. Goodbye, Miss Doolittle. (*They shake hands*).

Liza (*nodding to the others*). Goodbye, all.

Freddy (*opening the door for her*). Are you walking across the Park, Miss Doolittle? If so—

Liza (*with perfectly elegant diction*). Walk! Not bloody likely. (*Sensation*) I am going in a taxi. (*She goes out*).

[PICKERING *gasps and sits down.* FREDDY *goes out on the balcony to catch another glimpse of* ELIZA.]

Mrs Eynsford Hill (*suffering from shock*). Well, I really cant get used to the new ways.

Clara (*throwing herself discontentedly into the Elizabethan chair*). Oh, it's all right, mamma, quite right. People will think we never go anywhere or see anybody if you are so old-fashioned.

Mrs Eynsford Hill. I daresay I am very old-fashioned; but I do hope you wont begin using that expression, Clara. I have got accustomed to hear you talking about men as rotters, and calling everything filthy and beastly; though I do think it horrible and unladylike. But this last is really too much. Dont you think so, Colonel Pickering?

Pickering. Dont ask me. Ive been away in India for several years; and manners have changed so much that I sometimes dont know whether I'm at a respectable dinner-table or in a ship's forecastle.[8]

Clara. It's all a matter of habit. Theres no right or wrong in it. Nobody means anything by it. And it's so quaint, and gives such a smart emphasis to things that are not in themselves very witty. I find the new small talk delightful and quite innocent.

Mrs Eynsford Hill (*rising*). Well, after that, I think it's time for us to go.

[PICKERING *and* HIGGINS *rise.*]

Clara (*rising*). Oh yes: we have three at-homes to go to still. Goodbye, Mrs Higgins. Goodbye, Colonel Pickering. Goodbye, Professor Higgins.

Higgins (*coming grimly at her from the divan, and accompanying her to the door*). Goodbye. Be sure you try on that small talk at the three at-homes. Dont be nervous about it. Pitch it in strong.

Clara (*all smiles*). I will. Goodbye. Such nonsense, all this early Victorian prudery!

Higgins (*tempting her*). Such damned nonsense!

Clara. Such bloody nonsense!

Mrs Eynsford Hill (*convulsively*). Clara!

Clara. Ha! ha! (*She goes out radiant, conscious of being thoroughly up to date, and is heard descending the stairs in a stream of silvery laughter*).

---

8. **forecastle** (fōk´s´l): area at the front of a merchant ship where the crew is housed.

Freddy (*to the heavens at large*). Well, I ask you— (*He gives it up, and comes to* MRS HIGGINS). Goodbye.

Mrs Higgins (*shaking hands*). Goodbye. Would you like to meet Miss Doolittle again?

Freddy (*eagerly*). Yes, I should, most awfully.

Mrs Higgins. Well, you know my days.

Freddy. Yes. Thanks awfully. Goodbye. (*He goes out*).

Mrs Eynsford Hill. Goodbye, Mr Higgins.

Higgins. Goodbye. Goodbye.

Mrs Eynsford Hill (*to* PICKERING). It's no use. I shall never be able to bring myself to use that word.

Pickering. Dont. It's not compulsory, you know. Youll get on quite well without it.

Mrs Eynsford Hill. Only, Clara is so down on me if I am not positively reeking with the latest slang. Goodbye.

Pickering. Goodbye. (*They shake hands*).

Mrs Eynsford Hill (*to* MRS HIGGINS). You mustnt mind Clara. (PICKERING, *catching from her lowered tone that this is not meant for him to hear, discreetly joins* HIGGINS *at the window*). We're so poor! and she gets so few parties, poor child! She doesnt quite know. (MRS HIGGINS, *seeing that her eyes are moist, takes her hand sympathetically and goes with her to the door*). But the boy is nice. Dont you think so?

Mrs Higgins. Oh, quite nice. I shall always be delighted to see him.

Mrs Eynsford Hill. Thank you, dear. Goodbye. (*She goes out*).

Higgins (*eagerly*). Well? Is Eliza presentable? (*He swoops on his mother and drags her to the ottoman, where she sits down in* ELIZA's *place with her son on her left*).

[PICKERING *returns to his chair on her right.*]

Mrs Higgins. You silly boy, of course she's not presentable. She's a triumph of your art and of her dressmaker's; but if you suppose for a moment that she doesnt give herself away in every sentence she utters, you must be perfectly cracked about her.

Pickering. But dont you think something might be done? I mean something to eliminate the sanguinary[9] element from her conversation.

Mrs Higgins. Not as long as she is in Henry's hands.

Higgins (*aggrieved*). Do you mean that my language is improper?

Mrs Higgins. No, dearest: it would be quite proper—say on a canal barge; but it would not be proper for her at a garden party.

Higgins (*deeply injured*). Well I must say—

Pickering (*interrupting him*). Come, Higgins: you must learn to know yourself. I havnt heard such language as yours since we used to review the volunteers in Hyde Park twenty years ago.

Higgins (*sulkily*). Oh, well, if you say so, I suppose I dont always talk like a bishop.

Mrs Higgins (*quieting* HENRY *with a touch*). Colonel Pickering: will you tell me what is the exact state of things in Wimpole Street?

Pickering (*cheerfully: as if this completely changed the subject*). Well, I have come to live there with Henry. We work together at my Indian Dialects; and we think it more convenient—

Mrs Higgins. Quite so. I know all about that: it's an excellent arrangement. But where does this girl live?

Higgins. With us, of course. Where should she live?

Mrs Higgins. But on what terms? Is she a servant? If not, what is she?

Pickering (*slowly*). I think I know what you mean, Mrs Higgins.

Higgins. Well, dash me if *I* do! Ive had to work at the girl every day for months to get her to her present pitch. Besides, she's useful. She knows where my things are, and remembers my appointments and so forth.

---

9. **sanguinary** (saŋ´gwi·ner´ē): bloody; a reference to Eliza's use of the slang word *bloody.*

Mrs Higgins. How does your housekeeper get on with her?

Higgins. Mrs Pearce? Oh, she's jolly glad to get so much taken off her hands; for before Eliza came, she used to have to find things and remind me of my appointments. But she's got some silly bee in her bonnet about Eliza. She keeps saying "You dont think, sir"; doesnt she, Pick?

Pickering. Yes: thats the formula. "You dont think, sir." Thats the end of every conversation about Eliza.

Higgins. As if I ever stop thinking about the girl and her confounded vowels and consonants. I'm worn out, thinking about her, and watching her lips and her teeth and her tongue, not to mention her soul, which is the quaintest of the lot.

Mrs Higgins. You certainly are a pretty pair of babies, playing with your live doll.

Higgins. Playing! The hardest job I ever tackled: make no mistake about that, mother. But you have no idea how frightfully interesting it is to take a human being and change her into a quite different human being by creating a new speech for her. It's filling up the deepest gulf that separates class from class and soul from soul.

Pickering (*drawing his chair closer to* MRS HIGGINS *and bending over to her eagerly*). Yes: it's enormously interesting. I assure you, Mrs Higgins, we take Eliza very seriously. Every week— every day almost—there is some new change. (*Closer again*) We keep records of every stage—dozens of gramophone disks and photographs—

Higgins (*assailing her at the other ear*). Yes, by George: it's the most absorbing experiment I ever tackled. She regularly fills our lives up: doesnt she, Pick?

Pickering. We're always talking Eliza.

Higgins. Teaching Eliza.

Pickering. Dressing Eliza.

Mrs Higgins. What!

Higgins. Inventing new Elizas.

Higgins. [*speaking together*] You know, she has the most extra-ordinary quickness of ear:

Pickering. I assure you, my dear Mrs Higgins, that girl

Higgins. just like a parrot. Ive tried her with every

Pickering. is a genius. She can play the piano quite beautifully.

Higgins. possible sort of sound that a human being can make—

Pickering. We have taken her to classical concerts and to music

Higgins. Continental dialects, African dialects, Hottentot

Pickering. halls; and it's all the same to her: she plays everything

Higgins. clicks, things it took me years to get hold of; and

Pickering. she hears right off when she comes home, whether it's

Higgins. she picks them up like a shot, right away, as if she had

Pickering. Beethoven and Brahms or Lehar and Lionel Monckton;

Higgins. been at it all her life.

Pickering. though six months ago, she'd never as much as touched a piano—

Mrs Higgins (*putting her fingers in her ears, as they are by this time shouting one another down with an intolerable noise*). Sh-sh-sh—sh! (*They stop*).

Pickering. I beg your pardon. (*He draws his chair back apologetically*).

Higgins. Sorry. When Pickering starts shouting nobody can get a word in edgeways.

Mrs Higgins. Be quiet, Henry. Colonel Pickering: dont you realize that when Eliza walked into Wimpole Street, something walked in with her?

Pickering. Her father did. But Henry soon got rid of him.

Mrs Higgins. It would have been more to the point if her mother had. But as her mother didnt something else did.

Pickering. But what?

Mrs Higgins (*unconsciously dating herself by the word*). A problem.

Pickering. Oh, I see. The problem of how to pass her off as a lady.

Higgins. I'll solve that problem. Ive half solved it already.

Mrs Higgins. No, you two infinitely stupid male creatures: the problem of what is to be done with her afterwards.

Higgins. I dont see anything in that. She can go her own way, with all the advantages I have given her.

Mrs Higgins. The advantages of that poor woman who was here just now! The manners and habits that disqualify a fine lady from earning her own living without giving her a fine lady's income! Is that what you mean?

Pickering (*indulgently, being rather bored*). Oh, that will be all right, Mrs Higgins. (*He rises to go*).

Higgins (*rising also*). We'll find her some light employment.

Pickering. She's happy enough. Dont you worry about her. Goodbye. (*He shakes hands as if he were consoling a frightened child, and makes for the door*).

Higgins. Anyhow, theres no good bothering now. The thing's done. Goodbye, mother. (*He kisses her, and follows* PICKERING).

Pickering (*turning for a final consolation*). There are plenty of openings. We'll do whats right. Goodbye.

Higgins (*to* PICKERING *as they go out together*). Let's take her to the Shakespear exhibition at Earlscourt.

Pickering. Yes: lets. Her remarks will be delicious.

Higgins. She'll mimic all the people for us when we get home.

Pickering. Ripping. (*Both are heard laughing as they go downstairs*).

Mrs Higgins (*rises with an impatient bounce, and returns to her work at the writing-table. She sweeps a litter of disarranged papers out of her way; snatches a sheet of paper from her stationery case;*

and tries resolutely to write. At the third line she gives it up; flings down her pen; grips the table angrily and exclaims). Oh, men! men!! men!!!

* * *

Clearly Eliza will not pass as a duchess yet; and Higgins's bet remains unwon. But the six months are not yet exhausted; and just in time Eliza does actually pass as a princess. For a glimpse of how she did it imagine an Embassy in London one summer evening after dark. The hall door has an awning and a carpet across the sidewalk to the kerb, because a grand reception is in progress. A small crowd is lined up to see the guests arrive.

A Rolls-Royce car drives up. Pickering in evening dress, with medals and orders, alights, and hands out Eliza, in opera cloak, evening dress, diamonds, fan, flowers and all accessories. Higgins follows. The car drives off; and the three go up the steps and into the house, the door opening for them as they approach.

Inside the house they find themselves in a spacious hall from which the grand staircase rises. On the left are the arrangements for the gentlemen's cloaks. The male guests are depositing their hats and wraps there.

On the right is a door leading to the ladies' cloakroom. Ladies are going in cloaked and coming out in splendor. Pickering whispers to Eliza and points out the ladies' room. She goes into it. Higgins and Pickering take off their overcoats and take tickets for them from the attendant.

One of the guests, occupied in the same way, has his back turned. Having taken his ticket, he turns round and reveals himself as an important looking young man with an astonishingly hairy face. He has an enormous moustache, flowing out into luxuriant whiskers. Waves of hair cluster on his brow. His hair is cropped closely at the back, and glows with oil. Otherwise he is very smart. He wears several worthless orders. He is evidently a foreigner, guessable as a whiskered

Pandour[10] from Hungary; but in spite of the ferocity of his moustache he is amiable and genially voluble.

Recognizing Higgins, he flings his arms wide apart and approaches him enthusiastically.

Whiskers. Maestro, maestro. (*He embraces* Higgins *and kisses him on both cheeks*). You remember me?

Higgins. No I dont. Who the devil are you?

Whiskers. I am your pupil; your first pupil, your best and greatest pupil. I am little Nepommuck, the marvelous boy. I have made your name famous throughout Europe. You teach me phonetic. You cannot forget ME.

Higgins. Why don't you shave?

Nepommuck. I have not your imposing appearance, your chin, your brow. Nobody notice me when I shave. Now I am famous; they call me Hairy Faced Dick.

Higgins. And what are you doing here among all these swells?

Nepommuck. I am interpreter. I speak 32 languages. I am indispensable at these international parties. You are great cockney specialist: you place a man anywhere in London the moment he opens his mouth. I place any man in Europe.

[*A footman hurries down the grand staircase and comes to* Nepommuck.]

Footman. You are wanted upstairs. Her Excellency cannot understand the Greek gentleman.

Nepommuck. Thank you, yes, immediately.

[*The footman goes and is lost in the crowd.*]

Nepommuck (*to* Higgins). This Greek diplomatist pretends he cannot speak nor understand English. He cannot deceive me. He is the son of a Clerkenwell watchmaker. He speaks English so villainously that he dare not utter a word of it

---

10. **Pandour** (pan´door´): member of a Croatian unit in the Austrian army in the eighteenth century, known for their brutality.

without betraying his origin. I help him to pretend; but I make him pay through the nose. I make them all pay. Ha ha! (*He hurries upstairs*).

Pickering. Is this fellow really an expert? Can he find out Eliza and blackmail her?

Higgins. We shall see. If he finds her out I lose my bet.

[ELIZA *comes from the cloakroom and joins them.*]

Pickering. Well, Eliza, now for it. Are you ready?

Liza. Are you nervous, Colonel?

Pickering. Frightfully. I feel exactly as I felt before my first battle. It's the first time that frightens.

Liza. It is not the first time for me, Colonel. I have done this fifty times—hundreds of times—in my little piggery in Angel court in my day-dreams. I am in a dream now. Promise me not to let Professor Higgins wake me; for if he does I shall forget everything and talk as I used to in Drury Lane.

Pickering. Not a word, Higgins. (*To* ELIZA) Now, ready?

Liza. Ready.

Pickering. Go.

[*They mount the stairs,* HIGGINS *last.* PICKERING *whispers to the footman on the first landing.*]

First Landing Footman. Miss Doolittle, Colonel Pickering, Professor Higgins.

Second Landing Footman. Miss Doolittle, Colonel Pickering, Professor Higgins.

[*At the top of the staircase the Ambassador and his wife, with* NEPOMMUCK *at her elbow, are receiving.*]

Hostess (*taking* ELIZA's *hand*). How d'ye do?

Host (*same play*). How d'ye do? How d'ye do, Pickering?

Liza (*with a beautiful gravity that awes her hostess*). How do you do? (*She passes on to the drawing room*).

Hostess. Is that your adopted daughter, Colonel Pickering? She will make a sensation.

Pickering. Most kind of you to invite her for me. (*He passes on*).

Hostess (*to* NEPOMMUCK). Find out all about her.

Nepommuck (*bowing*). Excellency— (*He goes into the crowd*).

Host. How d'ye do, Higgins? You have a rival here tonight. He introduced himself as your pupil. Is he any good?

Higgins. He can learn a language in a fortnight—knows dozens of them. A sure mark of a fool. As a phonetician, no good whatever.

Hostess. How d'ye do, Professor?

Higgins. How do you do? Fearful bore for you this sort of thing. Forgive my part in it. (*He passes on*).

In the drawing room and its suite of salons the reception is in full swing. Eliza passes through. She is so intent on her ordeal that she walks like a somnambulist in a desert instead of a débutante in a fashionable crowd. They stop talking to look at her, admiring her dress, her jewels, and her strangely attractive self. Some of the younger ones at the back stand on their chairs to see.

The Host and Hostess come in from the staircase and mingle with their guests. Higgins, gloomy and contemptuous of the whole business, comes into the group where they are chatting.

Hostess. Ah, here is Professor Higgins: he will tell us. Tell us all about the wonderful young lady, Professor.

Higgins (*almost morosely*). What wonderful young lady?

Hostess. You know very well. They tell me there has been nothing like her in London since people stood on their chairs to look at Mrs Langtry.[11]

[NEPOMMUCK *joins the group, full of news*.]

Hostess. Ah, here you are at last, Nepommuck. Have you found out all about the Doolittle lady?

---

11. **Mrs Langtry:** Lillie Langtry (1853–1929), a famous and beautiful British actress.

Nepommuck. I have found out all about her. She is a fraud.

Hostess. A fraud! Oh no.

Nepommuck. YES, yes. She cannot deceive me. Her name cannot be Doolittle.

Higgins. Why?

Nepommuck. Because Doolittle is an English name. And she is not English.

Hostess. Oh, nonsense! She speaks English perfectly.

Nepommuck. Too perfectly. Can you shew me any English woman who speaks English as it should be spoken? Only foreigners who have been taught to speak it speak it well.

Hostess. Certainly she terrified me by the way she said How d'ye do. I had a schoolmistress who talked like that; and I was mortally afraid of her. But if she is not English what is she?

Nepommuck. Hungarian.

All the Rest. Hungarian!

Nepommuck. Hungarian. And of royal blood. I am Hungarian. My blood is royal.

Higgins. Did you speak to her in Hungarian?

Nepommuck. I did. She was very clever. She said "Please speak to me in English: I do not understand French." French! She pretended not to know the difference between Hungarian and French. Impossible: she knows both.

Higgins. And the blood royal? How did you find that out?

Nepommuck. Instinct, maestro, instinct. Only the Magyar races can produce that air of the divine right, those resolute eyes. She is a princess.

Host. What do you say, Professor?

Higgins. I say an ordinary London girl out of the gutter and taught to speak by an expert. I place her in Drury Lane.

Nepommuck. Ha ha ha! Oh maestro, maestro, you are mad on the subject of cockney dialects. The London gutter is the whole world for you.

Higgins (*to the* HOSTESS). What does your Excellency say?

Hostess. Oh, of course I agree with Nepommuck. She must be a princess at least.

Host. Not necessarily legitimate, of course. Morganatic[12] perhaps. But that is undoubtedly her class.
Higgins. I stick to my opinion.
Hostess. Oh, you are incorrigible.

[*The group breaks up, leaving* Higgins *isolated.* Pickering *joins him.*]

Pickering. Where is Eliza? We must keep an eye on her.

[Eliza *joins them.*]

Liza. I don't think I can bear much more. The people all stare so at me. An old lady has just told me that I speak exactly like Queen Victoria. I am sorry if I have lost your bet. I have done my best; but nothing can make me the same as these people.
Pickering. You have not lost it, my dear. You have won it ten times over.
Higgins. Let us get out of this. I have had enough of chattering to these fools.
Pickering. Eliza is tired; and I am hungry. Let us clear out and have supper somewhere.

---

12. **morganatic** (môr´gə·nat´ik): of a marriage between a member of a royal family and someone of lower rank. Children of such a marriage do not inherit titles or property from the royal parent.

Act IV

*The Wimpole Street laboratory. Midnight. Nobody in the room.
The clock on the mantelpiece strikes twelve. The fire is not alight: it
is a summer night.*

Presently HIGGINS *and* PICKERING *are heard on the stairs.*

Higgins (*calling down to* PICKERING). I say, Pick: lock up, will
you? I shant be going out again.
Pickering. Right. Can Mrs Pearce go to bed? We dont want
anything more, do we?
Higgins. Lord, no!

[ELIZA *opens the door and is seen on the lighted landing in all the
finery in which she has just won* HIGGINS's *bet for him. She comes
to the hearth, and switches on the electric lights there. She is tired:
her pallor contrasts strongly with her dark eyes and hair; and her
expression is almost tragic. She takes off her cloak; puts her fan and
gloves on the piano; and sits down on the bench, brooding and
silent.* HIGGINS, *in evening dress, with overcoat and hat, comes in,
carrying a smoking jacket which he has picked up downstairs. He
takes off the hat and overcoat; throws them carelessly on the news-
paper stand; disposes of his coat in the same way; puts on the smoking jacket; and throws himself wearily into the easy-chair at the
hearth.* PICKERING, *similarly attired, comes in. He also takes off his
hat and overcoat, and is about to throw them on* HIGGINS's *when he
hesitates.*]

Pickering. I say: Mrs Pearce will row if we leave these things
lying about in the drawing room.
Higgins. Oh, chuck them over the bannisters into the hall.
She'll find them there in the morning and put them away all
right. She'll think we were drunk.
Pickering. We are, slightly. Are there any letters?

Higgins. I didnt look. (PICKERING *takes the overcoats and hats and goes downstairs.* HIGGINS *begins half singing half yawning an air from* La Fanciulla del Golden West.[1] *Suddenly he stops and exclaims*) I wonder where the devil my slippers are!

[ELIZA *looks at him darkly; then rises suddenly and leaves the room.* HIGGINS *yawns again, and resumes his song.*
PICKERING *returns, with the contents of the letter-box in his hand.*]

Pickering. Only circulars, and this coroneted billet-doux [2] for you. (*He throws the circulars into the fender, and posts himself on the hearthrug, with his back to the grate*).
Higgins (*glancing at the billet-doux*). Money-lender. (*He throws the letter after the circulars*).

[ELIZA *returns with a pair of large down-at-heel slippers. She places them on the carpet before* HIGGINS, *and sits as before without a word.*]

Higgins (*yawning again*). Oh Lord! What an evening! What a crew! What a silly tomfoolery! (*He raises his shoe to unlace it, and catches sight of the slippers. He stops unlacing and looks at them as if they had appeared there of their own accord*). Oh theyre there, are they?
Pickering (*stretching himself*). Well, I feel a bit tired. It's been a long day. The garden party, a dinner party, and the reception! Rather too much of a good thing. But youve won your bet, Higgins. Eliza did the trick, and something to spare, eh?
Higgins (*fervently*). Thank God it's over!

[ELIZA *flinches violently; but they take no notice of her; and she recovers herself and sits stonily as before.*]

Pickering. Were you nervous at the garden party? *I* was. Eliza didnt seem a bit nervous.

---

1. **La Fanciulla del Golden West:** *La fanciulla del west (The Girl of the Golden West)*, an opera by the Italian composer Giacomo Puccini (1858–1924).
2. **billet-doux** (bē´yä doo´): love letter.

Higgins. Oh, she wasnt nervous. I knew she'd be all right. No: it's the strain of putting the job through all these months that has told on me. It was interesting enough at first, while we were at the phonetics; but after that I got deadly sick of it. If I hadnt backed myself to do it I should have chucked the whole thing up two months ago. It was a silly notion: the whole thing has been a bore.

Pickering. Oh come! the garden party was frightfully exciting. My heart began beating like anything.

Higgins. Yes, for the first three minutes. But when I saw we were going to win hands down, I felt like a bear in a cage, hanging about doing nothing. The dinner was worse: sitting gorging there for over an hour, with nobody but a damned fool of a fashionable woman to talk to! I tell you, Pickering, never again for me. No more artificial duchesses. The whole thing has been simple purgatory.

Pickering. Youve never been broken in properly to the social routine. (*Strolling over to the piano*) I rather enjoy dipping into it occasionally myself: it makes me feel young again. Anyhow, it was a great success: an immense success. I was quite frightened once or twice because Eliza was doing it so well. You see, lots of the real people cant do it at all: theyre such fools that they think style comes by nature to people in their position; and so they never learn. Theres always something professional about doing a thing superlatively well.

Higgins. Yes: thats what drives me mad: the silly people dont know their own silly business. (*Rising*) However, it's over and done with; and now I can go to bed at last without dreading tomorrow.

[ELIZA's *beauty becomes murderous.*]

Pickering. I think I shall turn in too. Still, it's been a great occasion: a triumph for you. Goodnight. (*He goes*).

Higgins (*following him*). Goodnight. (*Over his shoulder, at the door*) Put out the lights, Eliza; and tell Mrs Pearce not to make coffee for me in the morning: I'll take tea. (*He goes out*).

[ELIZA *tries to control herself and feel indifferent as she rises and walks across to the hearth to switch off the lights. By the time she gets there she is on the point of screaming. She sits down in* HIGGINS's *chair and holds on hard to the arms. Finally she gives way and flings herself furiously on the floor, raging.*]

Higgins (*in despairing wrath outside*). What the devil have I done with my slippers? (*He appears at the door*).

Liza (*snatching up the slippers, and hurling them at him one after the other with all her force*). There are your slippers. And there. Take your slippers; and may you never have a day's luck with them!

Higgins (*astounded*). What on earth—! (*He comes to her*). Whats the matter? Get up. (*He pulls her up*). Anything wrong?

Liza (*breathless*). Nothing wrong—with you. Ive won your bet for you, havnt I? Thats enough for you. *I* dont matter, I suppose.

Higgins. You won my bet! You! Presumptuous insect! *I* won it. What did you throw those slippers at me for?

Liza. Because I wanted to smash your face. I'd like to kill you, you selfish brute. Why didnt you leave me where you picked me out of—in the gutter? You thank God it's all over, and that now you can throw me back again there, do you? (*She crisps[3] her fingers frantically*).

Higgins (*looking at her in cool wonder*). The creature is nervous, after all.

Liza (*gives a suffocated scream of fury, and instinctively darts her nails at his face*)!!

Higgins (*catching her wrists*). Ah! would you? Claws in, you cat. How dare you shew your temper to me? Sit down and be quiet. (*He throws her roughly into the easy-chair*).

Liza (*crushed by superior strength and weight*). Whats to become of me? Whats to become of me?

Higgins. How the devil do I know whats to become of you? What does it matter what becomes of you?

---

3. **crisps:** curls.

Liza. You dont care. I know you dont care. You wouldnt care if I was dead. I'm nothing to you—not so much as them slippers.

Higgins (*thundering*). Those slippers.

Liza (*with bitter submission*). Those slippers. I didnt think it made any difference now.

[*A pause.* ELIZA *hopeless and crushed.* HIGGINS *a little uneasy.*]

Higgins (*in his loftiest manner*). Why have you begun going on like this? May I ask whether you complain of your treatment here?

Liza. No.

Higgins. Has anybody behaved badly to you? Colonel Pickering? Mrs Pearce? Any of the servants?

Liza. No.

Higgins. I presume you dont pretend that *I* have treated you badly?

Liza. No.

Higgins. I am glad to hear it. (*He moderates his tone*). Perhaps youre tired after the strain of the day. Will you have a glass of champagne? (*He moves towards the door*).

Liza. No. (*Recollecting her manners*) Thank you.

Higgins (*good-humored again*). This has been coming on you for some days. I suppose it was natural for you to be anxious about the garden party. But thats all over now. (*He pats her kindly on the shoulder. She writhes*). Theres nothing more to worry about.

Liza. No. Nothing more for you to worry about. (*She suddenly rises and gets away from him by going to the piano bench, where she sits and hides her face*). Oh God! I wish I was dead.

Higgins (*staring after her in sincere surprise*). Why? In heaven's name, why? (*Reasonably, going to her*) Listen to me, Eliza. All this irritation is purely subjective.

Liza. I dont understand. I'm too ignorant.

Higgins. It's only imagination. Low spirits and nothing else. Nobody's hurting you. Nothing's wrong. You go to bed like a good girl and sleep it off. Have a little cry and say your prayers: that will make you comfortable.

Liza. I heard your prayers. "Thank God it's all over!"

Higgins (*impatiently*). Well, dont you thank God it's all over? Now you are free and can do what you like.

Liza (*pulling herself together in desperation*). What am I fit for? What have you left me fit for? Where am I to go? What am I to do? Whats to become of me?

Higgins (*enlightened, but not at all impressed*). Oh, thats whats worrying you, is it? (*He thrusts his hands into his pockets, and walks about in his usual manner, rattling the contents of his pockets, as if condescending to a trivial subject out of pure kindness*). I shouldnt bother about it if I were you. I should imagine you wont have much difficulty in settling yourself somewhere or other, though I hadnt quite realized that you were going away. (*She looks quickly at him: he does not look at her, but examines the dessert stand on the piano and decides that he will eat an apple*). You might marry, you know. (*He bites a large piece out of the apple and munches it noisily*). You see, Eliza, all men are not confirmed old bachelors like me and the Colonel. Most men are the marrying sort (poor devils!); and youre not bad-looking: it's quite a pleasure to look at you sometimes—not now, of course, because youre crying and looking as ugly as the very devil; but when youre all right and quite yourself, youre what I should call attractive. That is, to the people in the marrying line, you understand. You go to bed and have a good nice rest; and then get up and look at yourself in the glass; and you wont feel so cheap.

[ELIZA *again looks at him, speechless, and does not stir.*

The look is quite lost on him: he eats his apple with a dreamy expression of happiness, as it is quite a good one.]

Higgins (*a genial afterthought occurring to him*). I daresay my mother could find some chap or other who would do very well.

Liza. We were above that at the corner of Tottenham Court Road.

Higgins (*waking up*). What do you mean?

Liza. I sold flowers. I didnt sell myself. Now youve made a lady of me I'm not fit to sell anything else. I wish youd left me where you found me.

Higgins (*slinging the core of the apple decisively into the grate*). Tosh, Eliza. Dont you insult human relations by dragging all this cant[4] about buying and selling into it. You neednt marry the fellow if you dont like him.

Liza. What else am I to do?

Higgins. Oh, lots of things. What about your old idea of a florist's shop? Pickering could set you up in one: he has lots of money. (*Chuckling*) He'll have to pay for all those togs you have been wearing today; and that, with the hire of the jewellery, will make a big hole in two hundred pounds. Why, six months ago you would have thought it the millennium[5] to have a flower shop of your own. Come! youll be all right. I must clear off to bed: I'm devilish sleepy. By the way, I came down for something: I forget what it was.

Liza. Your slippers.

Higgins. Oh yes, of course. You shied them at me. (*He picks them up, and is going out when she rises and speaks to him*).

Liza. Before you go, sir—

Higgins (*dropping the slippers in his surprise at her calling him Sir*). Eh?

Liza. Do my clothes belong to me or to Colonel Pickering?

Higgins (*coming back into the room as if her question were the very climax of unreason*). What the devil use would they be to Pickering?

Liza. He might want them for the next girl you pick up to experiment on.

Higgins (*shocked and hurt*). Is that the way you feel towards us?

Liza. I dont want to hear anything more about that. All I want to know is whether anything belongs to me. My own clothes were burnt.

Higgins. But what does it matter? Why need you start bothering about that in the middle of the night?

---

4. **cant:** insincere or meaningless talk.
5. **millennium:** golden age.

Liza. I want to know what I may take away with me. I dont want to be accused of stealing.

Higgins (*now deeply wounded*). Stealing! You shouldnt have said that, Eliza. That shews a want of feeling.

Liza. I'm sorry. I'm only a common ignorant girl; and in my station I have to be careful. There cant be any feelings between the like of you and the like of me. Please will you tell me what belongs to me and what doesn't?

Higgins (*very sulky*). You may take the whole damned houseful if you like. Except the jewels. Theyre hired. Will that satisfy you? (*He turns on his heel and is about to go in extreme dudgeon*).[6]

Liza (*drinking in his emotion like nectar, and nagging him to provoke a further supply*). Stop, please. (*She takes off her jewels*). Will you take these to your room and keep them safe? I dont want to run the risk of their being missing.

Higgins (*furious*). Hand them over. (*She puts them into his hands*). If these belonged to me instead of to the jeweller, I'd ram them down your ungrateful throat. (*He perfunctorily thrusts them into his pockets, unconsciously decorating himself with the protruding ends of the chains*).

Liza (*taking a ring off*). This ring isnt the jeweller's: it's the one you bought me in Brighton. I dont want it now. (HIGGINS *dashes the ring violently into the fireplace, and turns on her so threateningly that she crouches over the piano with her hands over her face, and exclaims*) Dont you hit me.

Higgins. Hit you! You infamous creature, how dare you accuse me of such a thing? It is you who have hit me. You have wounded me to the heart.

Liza (*thrilling with hidden joy*). I'm glad. Ive got a little of my own back, anyhow.

Higgins (*with dignity, in his finest professional style*). You have caused me to lose my temper: a thing that has hardly ever happened to me before. I prefer to say nothing more tonight. I am going to bed.

---

6. **dudgeon** (duj´ən): anger; resentment.

Liza (*pertly*). Youd better leave a note for Mrs Pearce about the coffee; for she wont be told by me.

Higgins (*formally*). Damn Mrs Pearce; and damn the coffee; and damn you; and (*wildly*) damn my own folly in having lavished my hard-earned knowledge and the treasure of my regard and intimacy on a heartless guttersnipe. (*He goes out with impressive decorum, and spoils it by slamming the door savagely*).

[ELIZA *goes down on her knees on the hearthrug to look for the ring. When she finds it she considers for a moment what to do with it. Finally she flings it down on the dessert stand and goes upstairs in a tearing rage.*]

* * *

The furniture of Eliza's room has been increased by a big wardrobe and a sumptuous dressing-table. She comes in and switches on the electric light. She goes to the wardrobe; opens it; and pulls out a walking dress, a hat, and a pair of shoes, which she throws on the bed. She takes off her evening dress and shoes; then takes a padded hanger from the wardrobe; adjusts it carefully in the evening dress; and hangs it in the wardrobe, which she shuts with a slam. She puts on her walking shoes, her walking dress, and hat. She takes her wrist watch from the dressing-table and fastens it on. She pulls on her gloves; takes her vanity bag; and looks into it to see that her purse is there before hanging it on her wrist. She makes for the door. Every movement expresses her furious resolution.

She takes a last look at herself in the glass.

She suddenly puts out her tongue at herself; then leaves the room, switching off the electric light at the door.

Meanwhile, in the street outside, Freddy Eynsford Hill, lovelorn, is gazing up at the second floor, in which one of the windows is still lighted.

The light goes out.

Freddy. Goodnight, darling, darling, darling.

[ELIZA *comes out, giving the door a considerable bang behind her.*]

Liza. Whatever are you doing here?

Freddy. Nothing. I spend most of my nights here. It's the only place where I'm happy. Dont laugh at me, Miss Doolittle.

Liza. Dont you call me Miss Doolittle, do you hear? Liza's good enough for me. (*She breaks down and grabs him by the shoulders*). Freddy: you dont think I'm a heartless guttersnipe, do you?

Freddy. Oh no, no, darling: how can you imagine such a thing? You are the loveliest, dearest—

[*He loses all self-control and smothers her with kisses. She, hungry for comfort, responds. They stand there in one another's arms.*

   An elderly police constable arrives.]

Constable (*scandalized*). Now then! Now then!! Now then!!!

[*They release one another hastily.*]

Freddy. Sorry, constable. Weve only just become engaged.

[*They run away.*]

The constable shakes his head, reflecting on his own courtship and on the vanity of human hopes. He moves off in the opposite direction with slow professional steps.

   The flight of the lovers takes them to Cavendish Square. There they halt to consider their next move.

Liza (*out of breath*). He didnt half give me a fright, that copper. But you answered him proper.

Freddy. I hope I havent taken you out of your way. Where were you going?

Liza. To the river.

Freddy. What for?

Liza. To make a hole in it.

Freddy (*horrified*). Eliza, darling. What do you mean? What's the matter?

Liza. Never mind. It doesnt matter now. There's nobody in the world now but you and me, is there?

Freddy. Not a soul.

[*They indulge in another embrace, and are again surprised by a much younger constable.*]

Second Constable. Now then, you two! What's this? Where do you think you are? Move along here, double quick.
Freddy. As you say, sir, double quick.

They run away again; and are in Hanover Square before they stop for another conference.

Freddy. I had no idea the police were so devilishly prudish.
Liza. It's their business to hunt girls off the streets.
Freddy. We must go somewhere. We cant wander about the streets all night.
Liza. Cant we? I think it'd be lovely to wander about for ever.
Freddy. Oh, darling.

[*They embrace again, oblivious of the arrival of a crawling taxi. It stops.*]

Taximan. Can I drive you and the lady anywhere, sir?

[*They start asunder.*]

Liza. Oh, Freddy, a taxi. The very thing.
Freddy. But, damn it, I've no money.
Liza. I have plenty. The Colonel thinks you should never go out without ten pounds in your pocket. Listen. We'll drive about all night; and in the morning I'll call on old Mrs Higgins and ask her what I ought to do. I'll tell you all about it in the cab. And the police wont touch us there.
Freddy. Righto! Ripping. (*To the taximan*) Wimbledon Common. (*They drive off*).

Act V

MRS HIGGINS's *drawing room. She is at her writing-table as before. The parlormaid comes in.*

The Parlormaid (*at the door*). Mr Henry, maam, is downstairs with Colonel Pickering.
Mrs Higgins. Well, shew them up.
The Parlormaid. Theyre using the telephone, maam. Telephoning to the police, I think.
Mrs Higgins. What!
The Parlormaid (*coming further in and lowering her voice*). Mr Henry's in a state, maam. I thought I'd better tell you.
Mrs Higgins. If you had told me that Mr Henry was not in a state it would have been more surprising. Tell them to come up when theyve finished with the police. I suppose he's lost something.
The Parlormaid. Yes, maam (*going*).
Mrs Higgins. Go upstairs and tell Miss Doolittle that Mr Henry and the Colonel are here. Ask her not to come down til I send for her.
The Parlormaid. Yes, maam.

[HIGGINS *bursts in. He is, as the parlormaid has said, in a state.*]

Higgins. Look here, mother: heres a confounded thing!
Mrs Higgins. Yes, dear. Good morning. (*He checks his impatience and kisses her, whilst the parlormaid goes out*). What is it?
Higgins. Eliza's bolted.[1]
Mrs Higgins (*calmly continuing her writing*). You must have frightened her.

---

1. **bolted:** run away.

Higgins. Frightened her! nonsense! She was left last night, as usual, to turn out the lights and all that; and instead of going to bed she changed her clothes and went right off: her bed wasnt slept in. She came in a cab for her things before seven this morning; and that fool Mrs Pearce let her have them without telling me a word about it. What am I to do?

Mrs Higgins. Do without, I'm afraid, Henry. The girl has a perfect right to leave if she chooses.

Higgins (*wandering distractedly across the room*). But I cant find anything. I dont know what appointments Ive got. I'm— (PICKERING *comes in.* MRS HIGGINS *puts down her pen and turns away from the writing-table*).

Pickering (*shaking hands*). Good morning, Mrs Higgins. Has Henry told you? (*He sits down on the ottoman*).

Higgins. What does that ass of an inspector say? Have you offered a reward?

Mrs Higgins (*rising in indignant amazement*). You dont mean to say you have set the police after Eliza?

Higgins. Of course. What are the police for? What else could we do? (*He sits in the Elizabethan chair*).

Pickering. The inspector made a lot of difficulties. I really think he suspected us of some improper purpose.

Mrs Higgins. Well, of course he did. What right have you to go to the police and give the girl's name as if she were a thief, or a lost umbrella, or something? Really! (*She sits down again, deeply vexed*).

Higgins. But we want to find her.

Pickering. We cant let her go like this, you know, Mrs Higgins. What were we to do?

Mrs Higgins. You have no more sense, either of you, than two children. Why—

[*The parlormaid comes in and breaks off the conversation.*]

The Parlormaid. Mr Henry: a gentleman wants to see you very particular. He's been sent on from Wimpole Street.

Higgins. Oh, bother! I cant see anyone now. Who is it?

The Parlormaid. A Mr Doolittle, sir.

Pickering. Doolittle! Do you mean the dustman?

The Parlormaid. Dustman! Oh no, sir: a gentleman.

Higgins (*springing up excitedly*). By George, Pick, it's some relative of hers that she's gone to. Somebody we know nothing about. (*To the parlormaid*) Send him up, quick.

The Parlormaid. Yes, sir. (*She goes*).

Higgins (*eagerly, going to his mother*). Genteel relatives! now we shall hear something. (*He sits down in the Chippendale chair*).

Mrs Higgins. Do you know any of her people?

Pickering. Only her father: the fellow we told you about.

The Parlormaid (*announcing*). Mr Doolittle. (*She withdraws*).

[DOOLITTLE *enters. He is resplendently dressed as for a fashionable wedding, and might, in fact, be the bridegroom. A flower in his buttonhole, a dazzling silk hat, and patent leather shoes complete the effect. He is too concerned with the business he has come on to notice* MRS HIGGINS. *He walks straight to* HIGGINS, *and accosts him with vehement reproach.*]

Doolittle (*indicating his own person*). See here! Do you see this? You done this.

Higgins. Done what, man?

Doolittle. This, I tell you. Look at it. Look at this hat. Look at this coat.

Pickering. Has Eliza been buying you clothes?

Doolittle. Eliza! not she. Why would she buy me clothes?

Mrs Higgins. Good morning, Mr Doolittle. Wont you sit down?

Doolittle (*taken aback as he becomes conscious that he has forgotten his hostess*). Asking your pardon, maam. (*He approaches her and shakes her proffered hand*). Thank you. (*He sits down on the ottoman, on* PICKERING's *right*). I am that full of what has happened to me that I cant think of anything else.

Higgins. What the dickens has happened to you?

Doolittle. I shouldnt mind if it had only happened to me: anything might happen to anybody and nobody to blame but

Providence, as you might say. But this is something that you done to me: yes, you, Enry Iggins.

Higgins. Have you found Eliza?

Doolittle. Have you lost her?

Higgins. Yes.

Doolittle. You have all the luck, you have. I aint found her; but she'll find me quick enough now after what you done to me.

Mrs Higgins. But what has my son done to you, Mr Doolittle?

Doolittle. Done to me! Ruined me. Destroyed my happiness. Tied me up and delivered me into the hands of middle class morality.

Higgins (*rising intolerantly and standing over* DOOLITTLE). Youre raving. Youre drunk. Youre mad. I gave you five pounds. After that I had two conversations with you, at half-a-crown an hour. Ive never seen you since.

Doolittle. Oh! Drunk am I? Mad am I? Tell me this. Did you or did you not write a letter to an old blighter in America that was giving five millions to found Moral Reform Societies all over the world, and that wanted you to invent a universal language for him?

Higgins. What! Ezra D. Wannafeller! He's dead. (*He sits down again carelessly*).

Doolittle. Yes: he's dead; and I'm done for. Now did you or did you not write a letter to him to say that the most original moralist at present in England, to the best of your knowledge, was Alfred Doolittle, a common dustman?

Higgins. Oh, after your first visit I remember making some silly joke of the kind.

Doolittle. Ah! You may well call it a silly joke. It put the lid on me right enough. Just give him the chance he wanted to shew that Americans is not like us: that they reckonize and respect merit in every class of life, however humble. Them words is in his blooming will, in which, Henry Higgins, thanks to your silly joking, he leaves me a share in his Pre-digested Cheese Trust worth three thousand a year on condition that I lecture for his Wannafeller Moral Reform World League as often as they ask me up to six times a year.

Higgins. The devil he does! Whew! (*Brightening suddenly*) What a lark!

Pickering. A safe thing for you, Doolittle. They wont ask you twice.

Doolittle. It aint the lecturing I mind. I'll lecture them blue in the face, I will, and not turn a hair. It's making a gentleman of me that I object to. Who asked him to make a gentleman of me? I was happy. I was free. I touched pretty nigh everybody for money when I wanted it, same as I touched you, Enry Iggins. Now I am worrited; tied neck and heels; and everybody touches me for money. It's a fine thing for you, says my solicitor.[2] Is it? says I. You mean it's a good thing for you, I says. When I was a poor man and had a solicitor once when they found a pram[3] in the dust cart, he got me off, and got shut of me and got me shut of him as quick as he could. Same with the doctors: used to shove me out of the hospital before I could hardly stand on my legs, and nothing to pay. Now they find out that I'm not a healthy man and cant live unless they looks after me twice a day. In the house I'm not let do a hand's turn for myself: somebody else must do it and touch me for it. A year ago I hadnt a relative in the world except two or three that wouldnt speak to me. Now Ive fifty, and not a decent week's wages among the lot of them. I have to live for others and not for myself: thats middle class morality. You talk of losing Eliza. Dont you be anxious: I bet she's on my doorstep by this: she that could support herself easy by selling flowers if I wasnt respectable. And the next one to touch me will be you, Enry Iggins. I'll have to learn to speak middle class language from you, instead of speaking proper English. Thats where youll come in; and I daresay thats what you done it for.

---

2. **solicitor:** lawyer.
3. **pram:** British for "baby carriage."

Mrs Higgins. But, my dear Mr Doolittle, you need not suffer all this if you are really in earnest. Nobody can force you to accept this bequest. You can repudiate it. Isnt that so, Colonel Pickering?

Pickering. I believe so.

Doolittle (*softening his manner in deference to her sex*). Thats the tragedy of it, maam. It's easy to say chuck it; but I havent the nerve. Which of us has? We're all intimidated. Intimidated, maam: thats what we are. What is there for me if I chuck it but the workhouse in my old age? I have to dye my hair already to keep my job as a dustman. If I was one of the deserving poor, and had put by a bit, I could chuck it; but then why should I, acause the deserving poor might as well be millionaires for all the happiness they ever has. They dont know what happiness is. But I, as one of the undeserving poor, have nothing between me and the pauper's uniform but this here blasted three thousand a year that shoves me into the middle class. (Excuse the expression, maam; youd use it yourself if you had my provocation). Theyve got you every way you turn: it's a choice between the Skilly of the workhouse and the Char Bydis[4] of the middle class; and I havnt the nerve for the workhouse. Intimidated: thats what I am. Broke. Bought up. Happier men than me will call for my dust, and touch me for their tip; and I'll look on helpless, and envy them. And thats what your son has brought me to. (*He is overcome by emotion*).

Mrs Higgins. Well, I'm very glad youre not going to do anything foolish, Mr Doolittle. For this solves the problem of Eliza's future. You can provide for her now.

Doolittle (*with melancholy resignation*). Yes, maam: I'm expected to provide for everyone now, out of three thousand a year.

---

4. **Skilly . . . Char Bydis:** reference to Scylla (sil´ə), a large rock, and Charybdis (kə·rib´dis), a whirlpool, in the straits between Sicily and the Italian mainland. To "sail between Scylla and Charybdis" means to be caught between two dangerous or difficult situations.

Higgins (*jumping up*). Nonsense! he cant provide for her. He shant provide for her. She doesnt belong to him. I paid him five pounds for her. Doolittle: either youre an honest man or a rogue.

Doolittle (*tolerantly*). A little of both, Henry, like the rest of us: a little of both.

Higgins. Well, you took that money for the girl; and you have no right to take her as well.

Mrs Higgins. Henry: dont be absurd. If you want to know where Eliza is, she is upstairs.

Higgins (*amazed*). Upstairs!!! Then I shall jolly soon fetch her downstairs. (*He makes resolutely for the door*).

Mrs Higgins (*rising and following him*). Be quiet, Henry. Sit down.

Higgins. I—

Mrs Higgins. Sit down, dear; and listen to me.

Higgins. Oh very well, very well, very well. (*He throws himself ungraciously on the ottoman, with his face towards the windows*). But I think you might have told us this half an hour ago.

Mrs Higgins. Eliza came to me this morning. She told me of the brutal way you two treated her.

Higgins (*bounding up again*). What!

Pickering (*rising also*). My dear Mrs Higgins, she's been telling you stories. We didnt treat her brutally. We hardly said a word to her; and we parted on particularly good terms. (*Turning on* HIGGINS) Higgins: did you bully her after I went to bed?

Higgins. Just the other way about. She threw my slippers in my face. She behaved in the most outrageous way. I never gave her the slightest provocation. The slippers came bang into my face the moment I entered the room—before I had uttered a word. And used perfectly awful language.

Pickering (*astonished*). But why? What did we do to her?

Mrs Higgins. I think I know pretty well what you did. The girl is naturally rather affectionate, I think. Isnt she, Mr Doolittle?

Doolittle. Very tender-hearted, maam. Takes after me.

Mrs Higgins. Just so. She had become attached to you both. She worked very hard for you, Henry. I dont think you quite realize what anything in the nature of brain work means to a girl of her class. Well, it seems that when the great day of trial came, and she did this wonderful thing for you without making a single mistake, you two sat there and never said a word to her, but talked together of how glad you were that it was all over and how you had been bored with the whole thing. And then you were surprised because she threw your slippers at you! *I* should have thrown the fire-irons at you.

Higgins. We said nothing except that we were tired and wanted to go to bed. Did we, Pick?

Pickering (*shrugging his shoulders*). That was all.

Mrs Higgins (*ironically*). Quite sure?

Pickering. Absolutely. Really, that was all.

Mrs Higgins. You didnt thank her, or pet her, or admire her, or tell her how splendid she'd been.

Higgins (*impatiently*). But she knew all about that. We didnt make speeches to her, if thats what you mean.

Pickering (*conscience stricken*). Perhaps we were a little inconsiderate. Is she very angry?

Mrs Higgins (*returning to her place at the writing-table*). Well, I'm afraid she wont go back to Wimpole Street, especially now that Mr Doolittle is able to keep up the position you have thrust on her; but she says she is quite willing to meet you on friendly terms and to let bygones be bygones.

Higgins (*furious*). Is she, by George? Ho!

Mrs Higgins. If you promise to behave yourself, Henry, I'll ask her to come down. If not, go home; for you have taken up quite enough of my time.

Higgins. Oh, all right. Very well. Pick: you behave yourself. Let us put on our best Sunday manners for this creature that we picked out of the mud. (*He flings himself sulkily into the Elizabethan chair*).

Doolittle (*remonstrating*). Now, now, Enry Iggins! Have some consideration for my feelings as a middle class man.

Mrs Higgins. Remember your promise, Henry. (*She presses the bell-button on the writing-table*). Mr Doolittle: will you be so good as to step out on the balcony for a moment. I dont want Eliza to have the shock of your news until she has made it up with these two gentlemen. Would you mind?

Doolittle. As you wish, lady. Anything to help Henry to keep her off my hands. (*He disappears through the window*).

[*The parlormaid answers the bell.* PICKERING *sits down in* DOOLITTLE's *place.*]

Mrs Higgins. Ask Miss Doolittle to come down, please.

The Parlormaid. Yes, maam. (*She goes out*).

Mrs Higgins. Now, Henry: be good.

Higgins. I am behaving myself perfectly.

Pickering. He is doing his best, Mrs Higgins.

[*A pause.* HIGGINS *throws back his head; stretches out his legs; and begins to whistle.*]

Mrs Higgins. Henry, dearest, you dont look at all nice in that attitude.

Higgins (*pulling himself together*). I was not trying to look nice, mother.

Mrs Higgins. It doesnt matter, dear. I only wanted to make you speak.

Higgins. Why?

Mrs Higgins. Because you cant speak and whistle at the same time.

[HIGGINS *groans. Another very trying pause.*]

Higgins (*springing up, out of patience*). Where the devil is that girl? Are we to wait here all day?

[ELIZA *enters, sunny, self-possessed, and giving a staggeringly convincing exhibition of ease of manner. She carries a little work-basket, and is very much at home.* PICKERING *is too much taken aback to rise.*]

Liza. How do you do, Professor Higgins? Are you quite well?

Higgins (*choking*). Am I— (*He can say no more*).

Liza. But of course you are: you are never ill. So glad to see you again, Colonel Pickering. (*He rises hastily; and they shake* *hands*). Quite chilly this morning, isnt it? (*She sits down on his left. He sits beside her*).

Higgins. Dont you dare try this game on me. I taught it to you; and it doesnt take me in. Get up and come home; and dont be a fool.

[ELIZA *takes a piece of needlework from her basket, and begins to stitch at it, without taking the least notice of this outburst.*]

Mrs Higgins. Very nicely put, indeed, Henry. No woman could resist such an invitation.

Higgins. You let her alone, mother. Let her speak for herself. You will jolly soon see whether she has an idea that I havnt put into her head or a word that I havnt put into her mouth. I tell you I have created this thing out of the squashed cabbage leaves of Covent Garden; and now she pretends to play the fine lady with me.

Mrs Higgins (*placidly*). Yes, dear; but youll sit down, wont you?

[HIGGINS *sits down again, savagely.*]

Liza (*to* PICKERING, *taking no apparent notice of* HIGGINS, *and working away deftly*). Will you drop me altogether now that the experiment is over, Colonel Pickering?

Pickering. Oh dont. You mustnt think of it as an experiment. It shocks me, somehow.

Liza. Oh, I'm only a squashed cabbage leaf—

Pickering (*impulsively*). No.

Liza (*continuing quietly*). —but I owe so much to you that I should be very unhappy if you forgot me.

Pickering. It's very kind of you to say so, Miss Doolittle.

Liza. It's not because you paid for my dresses. I know you are generous to everybody with money. But it was from you that I learnt really nice manners; and that is what makes one a lady, isnt it? You see it was so very difficult for me with the example of Professor Higgins always before me. I was brought up to be just like him, unable to control myself, and using bad language on the slightest provocation. And I should never have known that ladies and gentlemen didnt behave like that if you hadnt been there.

Higgins. Well!!

Pickering. Oh, thats only his way, you know. He doesnt mean it.

Liza. Oh, *I* didnt mean it either, when I was a flower girl. It was only my way. But you see I did it; and thats what makes the difference after all.

Pickering. No doubt. Still, he taught you to speak; and I couldnt have done that, you know.

Liza (*trivially*). Of course: that is his profession.

Higgins. Damnation!

Liza (*continuing*). It was just like learning to dance in the fashionable way: there was nothing more than that in it. But do you know what began my real education?

Pickering. What?

Liza (*stopping her work for a moment*). Your calling me Miss Doolittle that day when I first came to Wimpole Street. That was the beginning of self-respect for me. (*She resumes her stitching*). And there were a hundred little things you never noticed, because they came naturally to you. Things about standing up and taking off your hat and opening doors—

Pickering. Oh, that was nothing.

Liza. Yes: things that shewed you thought and felt about me as if I were something better than a scullery-maid; though of course I know you would have been just the same to a scullery-maid if she had been let into the drawing room. You never took off your boots in the dining room when I was there.

Pickering. You mustnt mind that. Higgins takes off his boots all over the place.

Liza. I know. I am not blaming him. It is his way, isnt it? But it made such a difference to me that you didnt do it. You see, really and truly, apart from the things anyone can pick up (the dressing and the proper way of speaking, and so on), the difference between a lady and a flower girl is not how she behaves, but how she's treated. I shall always be a flower girl to Professor Higgins, because he always treats me as a flower girl, and always will; but I know I can be a lady to you, because you always treat me as a lady, and always will.

Mrs Higgins. Please dont grind your teeth, Henry.

Pickering. Well, this is really very nice of you, Miss Doolittle.

Liza. I should like you to call me Eliza, now, if you would.

Pickering. Thank you. Eliza, of course.

Liza. And I should like Professor Higgins to call me Miss Doolittle.

Higgins. I'll see you damned first.

Mrs Higgins. Henry! Henry!

Pickering (*laughing*). Why dont you slang back at him? Dont stand it. It would do him a lot of good.

Liza. I cant. I could have done it once; but now I cant go back to it. You told me, you know, that when a child is brought to a foreign country, it picks up the language in a few weeks, and forgets its own. Well, I am a child in your country. I have forgotten my own language, and can speak nothing but yours. Thats the real break-off with the corner of Tottenham Court Road. Leaving Wimpole Street finishes it.

Pickering (*much alarmed*). Oh! but youre coming back to Wimpole Street, arnt you? Youll forgive Higgins?

Higgins (*rising*). Forgive! Will she, by George! Let her go. Let her find out how she can get on without us. She will relapse into the gutter in three weeks without me at her elbow.

[DOOLITTLE *appears at the centre window. With a look of dignified reproach at* HIGGINS, *he comes slowly and silently to his daughter, who, with her back to the window, is unconscious of his approach.*]

Pickering. He's incorrigible, Eliza. You wont relapse, will you?

Liza. No: not now. Never again. I have learnt my lesson. I dont believe I could utter one of the old sounds if I tried. (DOOLITTLE *touches her on her left shoulder. She drops her work, losing her self-possession utterly at the spectacle of her father's splendor*). A-a-a-a-a-ah-ow-ooh!

Higgins (*with a crow of triumph*). Aha! Just so. A-a-a-a-ahowooh! A-a-a-a-ahowooh! A-a-a-a-ahowooh! Victory! Victory! (*He throws himself on the divan, folding his arms, and spraddling arrogantly*).

Doolittle. Can you blame the girl? Dont look at me like that, Eliza. It aint my fault. Ive come into some money.

Liza. You must have touched a millionaire this time, dad.

Doolittle. I have. But I'm dressed something special today. I'm going to St George's, Hanover Square. Your stepmother is going to marry me.

Liza (*angrily*). Youre going to let yourself down to marry that low common woman!

Pickering (*quietly*). He ought to, Eliza. (*To* DOOLITTLE) Why has she changed her mind?

Doolittle (*sadly*). Intimidated, Governor. Intimidated. Middle class morality claims its victim. Wont you put on your hat, Liza, and come and see me turned off?

Liza. If the Colonel says I must, I—I'll (*almost sobbing*) I'll demean myself. And get insulted for my pains, like enough.

Doolittle. Dont be afraid: she never comes to words with anyone now, poor woman! respectability has broke all the spirit out of her.

Pickering (*squeezing* ELIZA's *elbow gently*). Be kind to them, Eliza. Make the best of it.

Liza (*forcing a little smile for him through her vexation*). Oh well, just to shew theres no ill feeling. I'll be back in a moment. (*She goes out*).

Doolittle (*sitting down beside* PICKERING). I feel uncommon nervous about the ceremony, Colonel. I wish youd come and see me through it.

Pickering. But youve been through it before, man. You were married to Eliza's mother.

Doolittle. Who told you that, Colonel?

Pickering. Well, nobody told me. But I concluded—naturally—

Doolittle. No: that aint the natural way, Colonel: it's only the middle class way. My way was always the undeserving way.

But dont say nothing to Eliza. She dont know: I always had a delicacy about telling her.

Pickering. Quite right. We'll leave it so, if you dont mind.

Doolittle. And youll come to the church, Colonel, and put me through straight?

Pickering. With pleasure. As far as a bachelor can.

Mrs Higgins. May I come, Mr Doolittle? I should be very sorry to miss your wedding.

Doolittle. I should indeed be honored by your condescension, maam; and my poor old woman would take it as a tremenjous compliment. She's been very low, thinking of the happy days that are no more.

Mrs Higgins (*rising*). I'll order the carriage and get ready. (*The men rise, except* HIGGINS). I shant be more than fifteen minutes. (*As she goes to the door* ELIZA *comes in, hatted and buttoning her gloves*). I'm going to the church to see your father married, Eliza. You had better come in the brougham[5] with me. Colonel Pickering can go on with the bridegroom.

[MRS HIGGINS *goes out.* ELIZA *comes to the middle of the room between the centre window and the ottoman.* PICKERING *joins her.*]

Doolittle. Bridegroom! What a word! It makes a man realize his position, somehow. (*He takes up his hat and goes towards the door*).

Pickering. Before I go, Eliza, do forgive Higgins and come back to us.

Liza. I dont think dad would allow me. Would you, dad?

Doolittle (*sad but magnanimous*). They played you off very cunning, Eliza, them two sportsmen. If it had been only one of them, you could have nailed him. But you see, there was two; and one of them chaperoned the other, as you might say. (*To* PICKERING) It was artful of you, Colonel; but I bear no malice: I should have done the same myself. I been the victim of one woman after another all my life; and I dont grudge you

---

5. **brougham** (broͦom): closed horse-drawn carriage with the driver's seat outside.

two getting the better of Liza. I shant interfere. It's time for us to go, Colonel. So long, Henry. See you in St George's, Eliza. (*He goes out*).

Pickering (*coaxing*). Do stay with us, Eliza. (*He follows* DOOLITTLE).

[ELIZA *goes out on the balcony to avoid being alone with* HIGGINS. *He rises and joins her there. She immediately comes back into the room and makes for the door; but he goes along the balcony quickly and gets his back to the door before she reaches it.*]

Higgins. Well, Eliza, youve had a bit of your own back, as you call it. Have you had enough? and are you going to be reasonable? Or do you want any more?

Liza. You want me back only to pick up your slippers and put up with your tempers and fetch and carry for you.

Higgins. I havnt said I wanted you back at all.

Liza. Oh, indeed. Then what are we talking about?

Higgins. About you, not about me. If you come back I shall treat you just as I have always treated you. I cant change my nature; and I dont intend to change my manners. My manners are exactly the same as Colonel Pickering's.

Liza. Thats not true. He treats a flower girl as if she was a duchess.

Higgins. And I treat a duchess as if she was a flower girl.

Liza. I see. (*She turns away composedly, and sits on the ottoman, facing the window*). The same to everybody.

Higgins. Just so.

Liza. Like father.

Higgins (*grinning, a little taken down*). Without accepting the comparison at all points, Eliza, it's quite true that your father is not a snob, and that he will be quite at home in any station of life to which his eccentric destiny may call him. (*Seriously*) The great secret, Eliza, is not having bad manners or good manners or any other particular sort of manners, but having the same manner for all human souls: in short, behaving as if you were in Heaven, where there are no third-class carriages, and one soul is as good as another.

Liza. Amen. You are a born preacher.

Higgins (*irritated*). The question is not whether I treat you rudely, but whether you ever heard me treat anyone else better.

Liza (*with sudden sincerity*). I dont care how you treat me. I dont mind your swearing at me. I shouldnt mind a black eye: Ive had one before this. But (*standing up and facing him*) I wont be passed over.

Higgins. Then get out of my way; for I wont stop for you. You talk about me as if I were a motor bus.

Liza. So you are a motor bus: all bounce and go, and no consideration for anyone. But I can do without you: dont think I cant.

Higgins. I know you can. I told you you could.

Liza (*wounded, getting away from him to the other side of the ottoman with her face to the hearth*). I know you did, you brute. You wanted to get rid of me.

Higgins. Liar.

Liza. Thank you. (*She sits down with dignity*).

Higgins. You never asked yourself, I suppose, whether *I* could do without you.

Liza (*earnestly*). Dont you try to get round me. Youll have to do without me.

Higgins (*arrogant*). I can do without anybody. I have my own soul: my own spark of divine fire. But (*with sudden humility*) I shall miss you, Eliza. (*He sits down near her on the ottoman*). I have learnt something from your idiotic notions: I confess that humbly and gratefully. And I have grown accustomed to your voice and appearance. I like them, rather.

Liza. Well, you have both of them on your gramophone and in your book of photographs. When you feel lonely without me, you can turn the machine on. It's got no feelings to hurt.

Higgins. I cant turn your soul on. Leave me those feelings; and you can take away the voice and the face. They are not you.

Liza. Oh, you are a devil. You can twist the heart in a girl as easy as some could twist her arms to hurt her. Mrs Pearce warned me. Time and again she has wanted to leave you; and you always got round her at the last minute. And you dont care a bit for her. And you dont care a bit for me.

Higgins. I care for life, for humanity; and you are a part of it that has come my way and been built into my house. What more can you or anyone ask?

Liza. I wont care for anybody that doesnt care for me.

Higgins. Commercial principles, Eliza. Like (*reproducing her Covent Garden pronunciation with professional exactness*) s'yollin voylets [*selling violets*], isnt it?

Liza. Dont sneer at me. It's mean to sneer at me.

Higgins. I have never sneered in my life. Sneering doesnt become either the human face or the human soul. I am expressing my righteous contempt for Commercialism. I dont and wont trade in affection. You call me a brute because you couldnt buy a claim on me by fetching my slippers and finding my spectacles. You were a fool: I think a woman fetching a man's slippers is a disgusting sight: did I ever fetch your slippers? I think a good deal more of you for throwing them in my face. No use slaving for me and then saying you want to be cared for: who cares for a slave? If you come back, come back for the sake of good fellowship; for youll get nothing else. Youve had a thousand times as much out of me as I have out of you; and if you dare to set up your little dog's tricks of fetching and carrying slippers against my creation of a Duchess Eliza, I'll slam the door in your silly face.

Liza. What did you do it for if you didnt care for me?

Higgins (*heartily*). Why, because it was my job.

Liza. You never thought of the trouble it would make for me.

Higgins. Would the world ever have been made if its maker had been afraid of making trouble? Making life means making trouble. Theres only one way of escaping trouble; and thats killing things. Cowards, you notice, are always shrieking to have troublesome people killed.

Liza. I'm no preacher: I dont notice things like that. I notice that you dont notice me.

Higgins (*jumping up and walking about intolerantly*). Eliza: youre an idiot. I waste the treasures of my Miltonic mind by spreading them before you. Once for all, understand that I go my way and do my work without caring twopence what happens to either of us. I am not intimidated, like your father and your stepmother. So you can come back or go to the devil: which you please.

Liza. What am I to come back for?

Higgins (*bouncing up on his knees on the ottoman and leaning over it to her*). For the fun of it. Thats why I took you on.

Liza (*with averted face*). And you may throw me out tomorrow if I dont do everything you want me to?

Higgins. Yes; and you may walk out tomorrow if I dont do everything you want me to.

Liza. And live with my stepmother?

Higgins. Yes, or sell flowers.

Liza. Oh! if I only could go back to my flower basket! I should be independent of both you and father and all the world! Why did you take my independence from me? Why did I give it up? I'm a slave now, for all my fine clothes.

Higgins. Not a bit. I'll adopt you as my daughter and settle money on you if you like. Or would you rather marry Pickering?

Liza (*looking fiercely round at him*). I wouldnt marry you if you asked me; and youre nearer my age than what he is.

Higgins (*gently*). Than he is: not "than what he is."

Liza (*losing her temper and rising*). I'll talk as I like. Youre not my teacher now.

Higgins (*reflectively*). I dont suppose Pickering would, though. He's as confirmed an old bachelor as I am.

Liza. Thats not what I want; and dont you think it. Ive always had chaps enough wanting me that way. Freddy Hill writes to me twice and three times a day, sheets and sheets.

Higgins (*disagreeably surprised*). Damn his impudence! (*He recoils and finds himself sitting on his heels*).

Liza. He has a right to if he likes, poor lad. And he does love me.

Higgins (*getting off the ottoman*). You have no right to encourage him.

Liza. Every girl has a right to be loved.

Higgins. What! By fools like that?

Liza. Freddy's not a fool. And if he's weak and poor and wants me, may be he'd make me happier than my betters that bully me and dont want me.

Higgins. Can he make anything of you? Thats the point.

Liza. Perhaps I could make something of him. But I never thought of us making anything of one another; and you never think of anything else. I only want to be natural.

Higgins. In short, you want me to be as infatuated about you as Freddy? Is that it?

Liza. No I dont. Thats not the sort of feeling I want from you. And dont you be too sure of yourself or of me. I could have been a bad girl if I'd liked. Ive seen more of some things than you, for all your learning. Girls like me can drag gentlemen down to make love to them easy enough. And they wish each other dead the next minute.

Higgins. Of course they do. Then what in thunder are we quarrelling about?

Liza (*much troubled*). I want a little kindness. I know I'm a common ignorant girl, and you a book-learned gentleman; but I'm not dirt under your feet. What I done (*correcting herself*) what I did was not for the dresses and the taxis: I did it because we were pleasant together and I come—came—to care for you; not to want you to make love to me, and not forgetting the difference between us, but more friendly like.

Higgins. Well, of course. Thats just how I feel. And how Pickering feels. Eliza: youre a fool.

Liza. Thats not a proper answer to give me. (*She sinks on the chair at the writing-table in tears*).

Higgins. It's all youll get until you stop being a common idiot. If youre going to be a lady, youll have to give up feeling neglected if the men you know dont spend half their time snivelling over you and the other half giving you black eyes. If you cant stand the coldness of my sort of life, and the strain of it, go back to the gutter. Work til youre more a brute than a human being; and then cuddle and squabble and drink til you fall asleep. Oh, it's a fine life, the life of the gutter. It's real:

it's warm: it's violent: you can feel it through the thickest skin: you can taste it and smell it without any training or any work. Not like Science and Literature and Classical Music and Philosophy and Art. You find me cold, unfeeling, selfish, dont you? Very well: be off with you to the sort of people you like. Marry some sentimental hog or other with lots of money, and a thick pair of lips to kiss you with and a thick pair of boots to kick you with. If you cant appreciate what youve got, youd better get what you can appreciate.

Liza (*desperate*). Oh, you are a cruel tyrant. I cant talk to you: you turn everything against me: I'm always in the wrong. But you know very well all the time that youre nothing but a bully. You know I cant go back to the gutter, as you call it, and that I have no real friends in the world but you and the Colonel. You know well I couldnt bear to live with a low common man after you two; and it's wicked and cruel of you to insult me by pretending I could. You think I must go back to Wimpole Street because I have nowhere else to go but father's. But dont you be too sure that you have me under your feet to be trampled on and talked down. I'll marry Freddy, I will, as soon as I'm able to support him.

Higgins (*thunderstruck*). Freddy!!! that young fool! That poor devil who couldnt get a job as an errand boy even if he had the guts to try for it. Woman: do you not understand that I have made you a consort for a king?

Liza. Freddy loves me: that makes him king enough for me. I dont want him to work: he wasnt brought up to it as I was. I'll go and be a teacher.

Higgins. Whatll you teach, in heaven's name?

Liza. What you taught me. I'll teach phonetics.

Higgins. Ha! ha! ha!

Liza. I'll offer myself as an assistant to that hairyfaced Hungarian.

Higgins (*rising in a fury*). What! That impostor! that humbug! that toadying ignoramus! Teach him my methods! my discoveries! You take one step in his direction and I'll wring your neck. (*He lays hands on her*). Do you hear?

Liza (*defiantly non-resistant*). Wring away. What do I care? I knew youd strike me some day. (*He lets her go, stamping with rage at having forgotten himself, and recoils so hastily that he stumbles back into his seat on the ottoman*). Aha! Now I know how to deal with you. What a fool I was not to think of it before! You cant take away the knowledge you gave me. You said I had a finer ear than you. And I can be civil and kind to people, which is more than you can. Aha! (*purposely dropping her aitches to annoy him*) Thats done you, Enry Iggins, it az. Now I dont care that (*snapping her fingers*) for your bullying and your big talk. I'll advertize it in the papers that your duchess is only a flower girl that you taught, and that she'll teach anybody to be a duchess just the same in six months for a thousand guineas. Oh, when I think of myself crawling under your feet and being trampled on and called names, when all the time I had only to lift up my finger to be as good as you, I could just kick myself.

Higgins (*wondering at her*). You damned impudent slut, you! But it's better than snivelling; better than fetching slippers and finding spectacles, isnt it? (*Rising*) By George, Eliza, I said I'd make a woman of you; and I have. I like you like this.

Liza. Yes: you can turn round and make up to me now that I'm not afraid of you, and can do without you.

Higgins. Of course I do, you little fool. Five minutes ago you were like a millstone round my neck. Now youre a tower of strength: a consort battleship. You and I and Pickering will be three old bachelors instead of only two men and a silly girl.

[MRS HIGGINS *returns, dressed for the wedding.* ELIZA *instantly becomes cool and elegant.*]

Mrs Higgins. The carriage is waiting, Eliza. Are you ready?

Liza. Quite. Is the Professor coming?

Mrs Higgins. Certainly not. He cant behave himself in church. He makes remarks out loud all the time on the clergyman's pronunciation.

Liza. Then I shall not see you again, Professor. Goodbye. (*She goes to the door*).

Mrs Higgins (*coming to* HIGGINS). Goodbye, dear.

Higgins. Goodbye, mother. (*He is about to kiss her, when he recollects something*). Oh, by the way, Eliza, order a ham and a Stilton cheese, will you? And buy me a pair of reindeer gloves, number eights, and a tie to match that new suit of mine. You can choose the color. (*His cheerful, careless, vigorous voice shews that he is incorrigible*).

Liza (*disdainfully*). Number eights are too small for you if you want them lined with lamb's wool. You have three new ties that you have forgotten in the drawer of your washstand. Colonel Pickering prefers double Gloucester to Stilton; and you dont notice the difference. I telephoned Mrs Pearce this morning not to forget the ham. What you are to do without me I cannot imagine. (*She sweeps out*).

Mrs Higgins. I'm afraid youve spoilt that girl, Henry. I should be uneasy about you and her if she were less fond of Colonel Pickering.

Higgins. Pickering! Nonsense: she's going to marry Freddy. Ha ha! Freddy! Freddy!! Ha ha ha ha ha!!!!! (*He roars with laughter as the play ends*).

Epilogue

The rest of the story need not be shewn in action, and indeed, would hardly need telling if our imaginations were not so enfeebled by their lazy dependence on the ready-mades and reach-me-downs of the ragshop in which Romance keeps its stock of "happy endings" to misfit all stories. Now, the history of Eliza Doolittle, though called a romance because the transfiguration it records seems exceedingly improbable, is common enough. Such transfigurations have been achieved by hundreds of resolutely ambitious young women since Nell Gwynne set them the example by playing queens and fascinating kings in the theatre in which she began by selling oranges. Nevertheless, people in all directions have assumed, for no other reason than that she became the heroine of a romance, that she must have married the hero of it. This is unbearable, not only because her little drama, if acted on such a thoughtless assumption, must be spoiled, but because the true sequel is patent to anyone with a sense of human nature in general, and of feminine instinct in particular.

Eliza, in telling Higgins she would not marry him if he asked her, was not coquetting: she was announcing a well-considered decision. When a bachelor interests, and dominates, and teaches, and becomes important to a spinster, as Higgins with Eliza, she always, if she has character enough to be capable of it, considers very seriously indeed whether she will play for becoming that bachelor's wife, especially if he is so little interested in marriage that a determined and devoted woman might capture him if she set herself resolutely to do it. Her decision will depend a good deal on whether she is really free to choose; and that, again, will depend on her age and income. If she is at the end of her youth, and has no security for her livelihood, she will marry him because she must marry anybody who will provide for her. But at Eliza's age a good-looking girl does not feel that pressure: she feels free to pick and choose. She is therefore guided by her instinct in the matter. Eliza's instinct tells her not to marry Higgins. It does not tell her to give him up. It is not in the slightest doubt as to his remaining one of the strongest personal interests in her life. It would be very sorely strained if there was another woman likely to supplant her with him. But as she feels sure of him on that last point, she has no doubt at all as to her course, and would not have any, even if the difference of twenty years in age, which seems so great to youth, did not exist between them.

As our own instincts are not appealed to by her conclusion, let us see whether we cannot discover some reason in it. When Higgins excused his indifference to young women on the ground that they had an irresistible rival in his mother, he gave the clue to his inveterate old-bachelordom. The case is uncommon only to the extent that remarkable mothers are uncommon. If an imaginative boy has a sufficiently rich mother who has intelligence, personal grace, dignity of character without harshness, and a cultivated sense of the best art of her time to enable her to make her house beautiful, she sets a standard for him against which very few women can struggle, besides effecting for him a disengagement of his affections, his sense of beauty, and his idealism from his specifically sexual impulses. This makes him a standing puzzle to the huge number of uncultivated people who have been brought up in tasteless homes by commonplace or disagreeable parents, and to whom, consequently, literature, painting, sculpture, music, and affectionate personal relations come as modes of sex if they come at all. The word passion means nothing else to them; and that Higgins could have a passion for phonetics and idealize his mother instead of Eliza, would seem to them absurd and unnatural. Nevertheless, when we look round and see that hardly anyone is too ugly or disagreeable to find a wife or a husband if he or she wants one, whilst many old maids and bachelors are above the average in quality and culture, we cannot help suspecting that the disentanglement of sex from the associations with which it is commonly confused, a disentanglement which persons of genius achieve by sheer intellectual analysis, is sometimes produced or aided by parental fascination.

Now, though Eliza was incapable of thus explaining to herself Higgins's formidable powers of resistance to the charm that prostrated Freddy at the first glance, she was instinctively aware that she could never obtain a complete grip of him, or come between him and his mother (the first necessity of the married woman). To put it shortly, she knew that for some mysterious reason he had not the makings of a married man in him, according to her conception of a husband as one to whom she would be his nearest and fondest and warmest interest. Even had there been no mother-rival, she would still have refused to accept an interest in herself that was secondary to philosophic interests. Had Mrs Higgins died, there would still have been Milton and the Universal Alphabet. Landor's remark that to those who have the greatest power of loving, love is a secondary affair, would not have recommended Landor to Eliza. Put that along with her resentment of Higgins's domineering superiority, and her mistrust of his coaxing cleverness in getting round her and evading her wrath when he had gone too far with his impetuous bullying, and you will see that Eliza's instinct had good grounds for warning her not to marry her Pygmalion.

And now, whom did Eliza marry? For if Higgins was a predestinate old bachelor, she was most certainly not a predestinate old maid. Well, that can be told very shortly to those who have not guessed it from the indications she has herself given them.

Almost immediately after Eliza is stung into proclaiming her considered determination not to marry Higgins, she mentions the fact that young Mr Frederick Eynsford Hill is pouring out his love for her daily through the post. Now Freddy is young, practically twenty years younger than Higgins: he is a gentleman (or, as Eliza would qualify him, a toff), and speaks like one. He is nicely dressed, is treated by the Colonel as an equal, loves her unaffectedly, and is not her master, nor ever likely to dominate her in spite of his advantage of social standing. Eliza has no use for the foolish romantic tradition that all women love to be mastered, if not actually bullied and beaten. "When you go to women" says Nietzsche[1] "take your whip with you." Sensible despots have never confined that precaution to women: they have taken their whips with them when they have dealt with men, and been slavishly idealized by the men over whom they have flourished the whip much more than by women. No doubt there are slavish women as well as slavish men; and women, like men, admire those that are stronger than themselves. But to admire a strong person and to live under that strong person's thumb are two different things. The weak may not be admired and hero-worshipped; but they are by no means disliked or shunned; and they never seem to have the least difficulty in marrying people who are too good for them. They may fail in emergencies; but life is not one long emergency: it is mostly a string of situations for which no exceptional strength is needed, and with which even rather weak people can cope if they have a stronger partner to help them out. Accordingly, it is a truth everywhere in evidence that strong people, masculine or feminine, not only do not marry stronger people, but do not shew any preference for them in selecting their friends. When a lion meets another with a louder roar "the first lion thinks the last a bore." The man or woman who feels strong enough for two, seeks for every other quality in a partner than strength.

The converse is also true. Weak people want to marry strong people who do not frighten them too much; and this often leads them to make the mistake we describe metaphorically as "biting off more than they can chew." They want too

---

1. **Nietzsche:** Friedrich Nietzsche (frē´driH´ nē´chə) (1844–1900), a German philosopher.

much for too little; and when the bargain is unreasonable beyond all bearing, the union becomes impossible: it ends in the weaker party being either discarded or borne as a cross, which is worse. People who are not only weak, but silly or obtuse as well, are often in these difficulties.

This being the state of human affairs, what is Eliza fairly sure to do when she is placed between Freddy and Higgins? Will she look forward to a lifetime of fetching Higgins's slippers or to a lifetime of Freddy fetching hers? There can be no doubt about the answer. Unless Freddy is biologically repulsive to her, and Higgins biologically attractive to a degree that overwhelms all her other instincts, she will, if she marries either of them, marry Freddy.

And that is just what Eliza did.

Complications ensued; but they were economic, not romantic. Freddy had no money and no occupation. His mother's jointure,[2] a last relic of the opulence of Largelady Park, had enabled her to struggle along in Earlscourt with an air of gentility, but not to procure any serious secondary education for her children, much less give the boy a profession. A clerkship at thirty shillings a week was beneath Freddy's dignity, and extremely distasteful to him besides. His prospects consisted of a hope that if he kept up appearances somebody would do something for him. The something appeared vaguely to his imagination as a private secretaryship or a sinecure[3] of some sort. To his mother it perhaps appeared as a marriage to some lady of means who could not resist her boy's niceness. Fancy her feelings when he married a flower girl who had become disclassed under extraordinary circumstances which were now notorious!

It is true that Eliza's situation did not seem wholly ineligible. Her father, though formerly a dustman, and now fantastically disclassed, had become extremely popular in the

---

2. **jointure:** property transferred by a man to his wife to be used after his death.

3. **sinecure** (si´nə·kyoor´): job that involves little work.

smartest society by a social talent which triumphed over every prejudice and every disadvantage. Rejected by the middle class, which he loathed, he had shot up at once into the highest circles by his wit, his dustmanship (which he carried like a banner), and his Nietzschean transcendence of good and evil. At intimate ducal dinners he sat on the right hand of the Duchess; and in country houses he smoked in the pantry and was made much of by the butler when he was not feeding in the dining room and being consulted by cabinet ministers. But he found it almost as hard to do all this on four thousand a year as Mrs Eynsford Hill to live in Earlscourt on an income so pitiably smaller that I have not the heart to disclose its exact figure. He absolutely refused to add the last straw to his burden by contributing to Eliza's support.

Thus Freddy and Eliza, now Mr and Mrs Eynsford Hill, would have spent a penniless honeymoon but for a wedding present of £500 from the Colonel to Eliza. It lasted a long time because Freddy did not know how to spend money, never having had any to spend, and Eliza, socially trained by a pair of old bachelors, wore her clothes as long as they held together and looked pretty, without the least regard to their being many months out of fashion. Still, £500 will not last two young people for ever; and they both knew, and Eliza felt as well, that they must shift for themselves in the end. She could quarter herself on Wimpole Street because it had come to be her home; but she was quite aware that she ought not to quarter Freddy there, and that it would not be good for his character if she did.

Not that the Wimpole Street bachelors objected. When she consulted them, Higgins declined to be bothered about her housing problem when that solution was so simple. Eliza's desire to have Freddy in the house with her seemed of no more importance than if she had wanted an extra piece of bedroom furniture. Pleas as to Freddy's character, and the moral obligation on him to earn his own living, were lost on Higgins. He denied that Freddy had any character, and declared that if he tried to do any useful work some competent person would have the trouble of undoing it: a procedure involving a net loss to the community, and great unhappiness to Freddy himself, who was obviously intended by Nature for such light work as amusing Eliza, which, Higgins declared, was a much more useful and honorable occupation than working in the city. When Eliza referred again to her project of teaching phonetics, Higgins abated not a jot of his violent opposition to it. He said she was not within ten years of being qualified to meddle with his pet subject; and as it was evident that the Colonel agreed with him, she felt she could not go against them in this grave matter, and that she had no right, without Higgins's consent, to exploit the knowledge he had given her; for his knowledge seemed to her as much his private property as his watch: Eliza was no communist. Besides, she was superstitiously devoted to them both, more entirely and frankly after her marriage than before it.

It was the Colonel who finally solved the problem, which had cost him much perplexed cogitation. He one day asked Eliza, rather shyly, whether she had quite given up her notion of keeping a flower shop. She replied that she had thought of it, but had put it out of her head, because the Colonel had said, that day at Mrs Higgins's, that it would never do. The Colonel confessed that when he said that, he had not quite recovered from the dazzling impression of the day before. They broke the matter to Higgins that evening. The sole comment vouchsafed by him very nearly led to a serious quarrel with Eliza. It was to the effect that she would have in Freddy an ideal errand boy.

Freddy himself was next sounded on the subject. He said he had been thinking of a shop himself; though it had presented itself to his pennilessness as a small place in which Eliza should sell tobacco at one counter whilst he sold newspapers at the opposite one. But he agreed that it would be extraordinarily jolly to go early every morning with Eliza to Covent Garden and buy flowers on the scene of their first meeting: a sentiment which earned him many kisses from his wife. He added that he had always been afraid to propose anything of the sort, because Clara would make an awful row about a step that must damage her matrimonial chances, and his mother could not be expected to like it after clinging for so many years to that step of the social ladder on which retail trade is impossible.

This difficulty was removed by an event highly unexpected by Freddy's mother. Clara, in the course of her incursions into those artistic circles which were the highest within her reach, discovered that her conversational qualifications were expected to include a grounding in the novels of Mr H. G. Wells.[4] She borrowed them in various directions so energetically that she swallowed them all within two months. The result was a conversion of a kind quite common today. A modern Acts of the Apostles[5] would fill fifty whole Bibles if anyone were capable of writing it.

Poor Clara, who appeared to Higgins and his mother as a disagreeable and ridiculous person, and to her own mother as in some inexplicable way a social failure, had never seen herself in either light; for, though to some extent ridiculed and mimicked in West Kensington like everybody else there, she was accepted as a rational and normal—or shall we say inevitable?—sort of human being. At worst they called her The Pusher; but to them no more than to herself had it ever occurred that she was pushing the air, and pushing it in a wrong direction. Still, she was not happy. She was growing desperate. Her one asset, the fact that her mother was what the Epsom greengrocer called a carriage lady, had no exchange value, apparently. It had prevented her from getting educated, because the only education she could have afforded was education with the Earlscourt greengrocer's daughter. It had led her to seek the society of her mother's class; and that class simply would not have her, because she

---

4. **H. G. Wells** (1866–1946): English novelist who advocated social reform in his writing.
5. **Acts of the Apostles:** book of the New Testament that describes the beginnings of the Christian Church and the spread of Christianity.

was much poorer than the greengrocer, and, far from being able to afford a maid, could not afford even a housemaid, and had to scrape along at home with an illiberally treated general servant. Under such circumstances nothing could give her an air of being a genuine product of Largelady Park. And yet its tradition made her regard a marriage with anyone within her reach as an unbearable humiliation. Commercial people and professional people in a small way were odious to her. She ran after painters and novelists; but she did not charm them; and her bold attempts to pick up and practise artistic and literary talk irritated them. She was, in short, an utter failure, an ignorant, incompetent, pretentious, unwelcome, penniless, useless little snob; and though she did not admit these disqualifications (for nobody ever faces unpleasant truths of this kind until the possibility of a way out dawns on them) she felt their effects too keenly to be satisfied with her position.

Clara had a startling eyeopener when, on being suddenly wakened to enthusiasm by a girl of her own age who dazzled her and produced in her a gushing desire to take her for a model, and gain her friendship, she discovered that this exquisite apparition had graduated from the gutter in a few months time. It shook her so violently, that when Mr H. G. Wells lifted her on the point of his puissant[6] pen, and placed her at the angle of view from which the life she was leading and the society to which she clung appeared in its true relation to real human needs and worthy social structure, he effected a conversion and a conviction of sin comparable to the most sensational feats of General Booth[7] or Gypsy Smith. Clara's snobbery went bang. Life suddenly began to move with her. Without knowing how or why, she began to make friends and enemies. Some of the acquaintances to whom she had been a tedious or indifferent or ridiculous affliction,

---

6. **puissant** (pyo͞oʹi·sənt): powerful.
7. **General Booth:** William Booth (1829–1912), an English religious leader; founder of the Salvation Army.

dropped her: others became cordial. To her amazement she found that some "quite nice" people were saturated with Wells, and that this accessibility to ideas was the secret of their niceness. People she had thought deeply religious, and had tried to conciliate on that tack with disastrous results, suddenly took an interest in her, and revealed a hostility to conventional religion which she had never conceived possible except among the most desperate characters. They made her read Galsworthy;[8] and Galsworthy exposed the vanity of Largelady Park and finished her. It exasperated her to think that the dungeon in which she had languished for so many unhappy years had been unlocked all the time, and that the impulses she had so carefully struggled with and stifled for the sake of keeping well with society, were precisely those by which alone she could have come into any sort of sincere human contact. In the radiance of these discoveries, and the tumult of their reaction, she made a fool of herself as freely and conspicuously as when she so rashly adopted Eliza's expletive in Mrs Higgins's drawing room; for the new-born Wellsian had to find her bearings almost as ridiculously as a baby; but nobody hates a baby for its ineptitudes, or thinks the worse of it for trying to eat the matches; and Clara lost no friends by her follies. They laughed at her to her face this time; and she had to defend herself and fight it out as best she could.

When Freddy paid a visit to Earlscourt (which he never did when he could possibly help it) to make the desolating announcement that he and his Eliza were thinking of blackening the Largelady scutcheon[9] by opening a shop, he found the little household already convulsed by a prior announcement from Clara that she also was going to work in an old furniture shop in Dover Street, which had been started by a fellow Wellsian. This appointment Clara owed, after all, to

---

8. **Galsworthy:** John Galsworthy (1867–1933), English novelist, playwright, and social critic.

9. **scutcheon:** coat of arms. The usual form of the word is *escutcheon*.

her old social accomplishment of Push. She had made up her mind that, cost what it might, she would see Mr Wells in the flesh; and she had achieved her end at a garden party. She had better luck than so rash an enterprise deserved. Mr Wells came up to her expectations. Age had not withered him, nor could custom stale his infinite variety in half an hour. His pleasant neatness and compactness, his small hands and feet, his teeming ready brain, his unaffected accessibility, and a certain fine apprehensiveness which stamped him as susceptible from his topmost hair to his tipmost toe, proved irresistible. Clara talked of nothing else for weeks and weeks afterwards. And as she happened to talk to the lady of the furniture shop, and that lady also desired above all things to know Mr Wells and sell pretty things to him, she offered Clara a job on the chance of achieving that end through her.

And so it came about that Eliza's luck held, and the expected opposition to the flower shop melted away. The shop is in the arcade of a railway station not very far from the Victoria and Albert Museum; and if you live in that neighborhood you may go there any day and buy a buttonhole from Eliza.

Now here is a last opportunity for romance. Would you not like to be assured that the shop was an immense success, thanks to Eliza's charms and her early business experience in Covent Garden? Alas! the truth is the truth: the shop did not pay for a long time, simply because Eliza and her Freddy did not know how to keep it. True, Eliza had not to begin at the very beginning: she knew the names and prices of the cheaper flowers; and her elation was unbounded when she found that Freddy, like all youths educated at cheap, pretentious, and thoroughly inefficient schools, knew a little Latin. It was very little, but enough to make him appear to her a Porson or Bentley, and to put him at his ease with botanical nomenclature. Unfortunately he knew nothing else; and Eliza, though she could count money up to eighteen shillings or so, and had acquired a certain familiarity with the language of Milton from her struggles to qualify herself for winning Higgins's bet, could not write out a bill without utterly disgracing the establishment. Freddy's power of stating in Latin that Balbus built a wall and that Gaul was divided into three parts[10] did not carry with it the slightest knowledge of accounts or business: Colonel Pickering had to explain to him what a cheque book and a bank account meant. And the pair were by no means easily teachable. Freddy backed up Eliza in her obstinate refusal to believe that they could save money by engaging a bookkeeper with some knowledge of the business. How, they argued, could you possibly save money by going to extra expense when you already could not make ends meet? But the Colonel, after making the ends meet over and over again, at last gently insisted; and Eliza, humbled to the dust by having to beg from him so often, and stung by the uproarious derision of Higgins, to whom the notion of Freddy succeeding at anything was a joke that never palled, grasped the fact that business, like phonetics, has to be learned.

On the piteous spectacle of the pair spending their evenings in shorthand schools and polytechnic classes, learning bookkeeping and typewriting with incipient junior clerks, male and female, from the elementary schools, let me not dwell. There were even classes at the London School of Economics, and a humble personal appeal to the director of that institution to recommend a course bearing on the flower business. He, being a humorist, explained to them the method of the celebrated Dickensian essay on Chinese Metaphysics by the gentleman who read an article on China and an article on Metaphysics and combined the information. He suggested that they should combine the London School with Kew Gardens. Eliza, to whom the procedure of the Dickensian gentleman seemed perfectly correct (as in fact it was) and not in the least funny (which was only her igno-

---

10. **Gaul ... parts:** reference to the opening sentence of an account of the Gallic Wars written by Julius Caesar and commonly read in advanced Latin classes.

rance), took the advice with entire gravity. But the effort that cost her the deepest humiliation was a request to Higgins, whose pet artistic fancy, next to Milton's verse, was caligraphy, and who himself wrote a most beautiful Italian hand, that he would teach her to write. He declared that she was congenitally incapable of forming a single letter worthy of the least of Milton's words; but she persisted; and again he suddenly threw himself into the task of teaching her with a combination of stormy intensity, concentrated patience, and occasional bursts of interesting disquisition on the beauty and nobility, the august mission and destiny, of human handwriting. Eliza ended by acquiring an extremely uncommercial script which was a positive extension of her personal beauty, and spending three times as much on stationery as anyone else because certain qualities and shapes of paper became indispensable to her. She could not even address an envelope in the usual way because it made the margins all wrong.

Their commercial schooldays were a period of disgrace and despair for the young couple. They seemed to be learning nothing about flower shops. At last they gave it up as hopeless, and shook the dust of the shorthand schools, and the polytechnics, and the London School of Economics from their feet for ever. Besides, the business was in some mysterious way beginning to take care of itself. They had somehow forgotten their objections to employing other people. They came to the conclusion that their own way was the best, and that they had really a remarkable talent for business. The Colonel, who had been compelled for some years to keep a sufficient sum on current account at his bankers to make up their deficits, found that the provision was unnecessary: the young people were prospering. It is true that there was not quite fair play between them and their competitors in trade. Their week-ends in the country cost them nothing, and saved them the price of their Sunday dinners; for the motor car was the Colonel's; and he and Higgins paid the hotel bills. Mr F. Hill, florist and greengrocer (they soon discovered that there was money in asparagus; and asparagus led to other vegetables), had an air which stamped the business as classy; and in private life he was still Frederick Eynsford Hill, Esquire. Not that there was any swank about him: nobody but Eliza knew that he had been christened Frederick Challoner. Eliza herself swanked like anything.

That is all. That is how it has turned out. It is astonishing how much Eliza still manages to meddle in the housekeeping at Wimpole Street in spite of the shop and her own family. And it is notable that though she never nags her husband, and frankly loves the Colonel as if she were his favorite daughter, she has never got out of the habit of nagging Higgins that was established on the fatal night when she won his bet for him. She snaps his head off on the faintest provocation, or on none. He no longer dares to tease her by assuming an abysmal inferiority of Freddy's mind to his own. He storms and bullies and derides; but she stands up to him so ruthlessly that the Colonel has to ask her from time to time to be kinder to Higgins; and it is the only request of his that brings a mulish expression into her face. Nothing but some emergency or calamity great enough to break down all likes and dislikes, and throw them both back on their common humanity—and may they be spared any such trial!—will ever alter this. She knows that Higgins does not need her, just as her father did not need her. The very scrupulousness with which he told her that day that he had become used to having her there, and dependent on her for all sorts of little services, and that he should miss her if she went away (it would never have occurred to Freddy or the Colonel to say anything of the sort) deepens her inner certainty that she is "no more to him than them slippers"; yet she has a sense, too, that his indifference is deeper than the infatuation of commoner souls. She is immensely interested in him. She has even secret mischievous moments in which she wishes she could get him alone, on a desert island, away from all ties and with nobody else in the world to consider, and just drag him off his pedestal and see him making love like any common man. We all have private imaginations of that sort. But when it comes to business, to the life that she really leads as distinguished from the life of dreams and fancies, she likes Freddy and she likes the Colonel; and she does not like Higgins and Mr Doolittle. Galatea never does quite like Pygmalion: his relation to her is too godlike to be altogether agreeable.[11]

11. In Greek mythology, **Pygmalion** (pig·māl´ē·ən) was a sculptor and king of Cyprus who fell in love with a statue of a woman he had carved. In response to his prayers, Aphrodite, the goddess of love, transformed the statue into a living woman, whom Pygmalion named **Galatea** (gal´ə·tē´ə).

A Commentary

A Critical Comment
by Robert Anderson

Pygmalion (1913) was Shaw's first popular success. Its original run in London was cut short by the beginning of World War I, but it was subsequently produced all over the world and finally emerged, in 1956, as the superb musical *My Fair Lady,* with lyrics by Alan Jay Lerner and music by Frederick Loewe.

People interested in the creative process are always asking writers, which came first, the story, the characters, or the theme? In *Pygmalion,* apparently, the juxtaposition of the two main characters came first. In an 1897 letter to the actress Ellen Terry, Shaw wrote:

> *Caesar and Cleopatra* has been driven clean out of my head by a play I want to write for them [the actors Johnston Forbes-Robertson and Mrs. Patrick Campbell] in which he shall be a West End gentleman and she an East End dona [a Spanish lady] in an apron and three orange and red ostrich feathers.

The facing off of two characters with opposite natures always makes for a good theatrical situation. But a situation does not make a play. The characters must be fleshed out, and for Shaw there had to be a message. In the Preface to an edition of *Pygmalion,* he boasts of the success of this didactic play, but Shaw must have known that its success was due to its appealing Cinderella theme and not to his preaching. (This same contrariness and irony reappeared years later, when Shaw was negotiating a contract with the famous Hollywood producer

Samuel Goldwyn. "The trouble, Mr. Goldwyn," said Shaw, "is that you are always thinking about art and I am thinking about money.")

The American playwright Howard Lindsay used to tell young playwrights that it's all right for a play to have a message, but the playwright shouldn't let the characters know about it. In other words, no ringing speeches should be made. Sam Goldwyn put it another way: "If you want to send a message, use Western Union."

Shaw had various messages, and he sent many of them via *Pygmalion*. The first message is about his arch enemy, the upper classes: By having an illiterate flower seller pass as a duchess just by learning how to speak and act properly, Shaw exposed the foolish pretensions of high society. In other words, class is only speech deep.

Later Eliza voices a more profound truth when she says to Pickering, "The difference between a lady and a flower girl is not how she behaves, but how she's treated."

The most serious message is expressed in Eliza's question: "Whats to become of me?" At the time this play was written, education in England was becoming increasingly available to all classes, but an educated flower girl would still be a flower girl: The class system made it difficult for her to find work commensurate with her education.

A final point seems to be a personal one for Shaw. In the face of Eliza's appeal that Higgins "care" for her, Shaw claims that the "superior" person should be allowed to pursue his or her high vocation without becoming enmeshed in emotions. This argument evokes the struggle of many an artist who has sought to achieve the solitude that creativity demands and still avoid the problem of loneliness. Shaw solved the problem for himself by making a friendly marriage in which, he said, emotion played no part.

For many people, Shaw's insistence on keeping Eliza and Higgins apart romantically almost ruins the play. They expect a play called *Pygmalion* to follow the general outlines of the Greek legend, in which the sculptor, Pygmalion, falls in love with the statue of a beautiful woman he has carved from marble. After asking the gods to bring her to life, he marries her.

The entire movement of *Pygmalion*, the tidal pull of the story, suggests that Cinderella will break down the reserve of her crusty prince and ride off with him into the sunset. But Shaw's message did not allow such an ending. And this was not just perversity on his part. Using his favorite device of anticlimax, Shaw meant to make a point, to shock us, to disappoint our expectations and make us hear his message. He wanted Eliza to be a liberated woman, who aspires to more than a conventional home life spent fetching her husband's slippers. Shaw meant us to rejoice in Eliza's freedom. (Most audiences, however, would rather have seen "girl gets boy.") Shaw might have constructed his story so that we would be eager for Eliza to go off on her own, but he didn't. He stuck with the charming story that demands a fairy-tale ending, then refused to provide it.

The actors playing Higgins, however, sometimes take matters into their own hands. The first actor to play the part of Higgins in London threw a rose after the departing Eliza at the play's end. The famous film of the play has Eliza return to Wimpole Street and fades out on actor Leslie Howard's loving smile as he watches her leave his study. *My Fair Lady*, the musical comedy based on the play, also ignores Shaw altogether, bringing Eliza and Higgins together in the end.

When Shaw was asked why he allowed a "happy ending" in the movie, he retorted,

> I did not. I cannot conceive a less happy ending to the story of *Pygmalion* than a love affair between the

middle-class professor, a confirmed bachelor with a mother fixation, and a flower girl of 18.

Change is at the heart of drama. In *Pygmalion* we watch the changes in Eliza and note the possibility of change in Higgins. (Whenever a character declares himself "a confirmed bachelor" in Act One, the audience members are bound to say to themselves, "We'll see about that.") The change in a character in a play is always rewarding, but when a main character changes, in Cinderella fashion, from guttersnipe to duchess, the audience is enraptured. This transformation of the "plain girl" into a beauty has by now been the basis of so many plays and movies that it has almost become a cliché.

Once Shaw put the flower seller together with the West End phonetics teacher, the story practically wrote itself: Girl wants to improve herself; teacher thinks it a joke to pass her off as a duchess. The obstacles are the basic difficulty of the task and Eliza's unwillingness to be bossed around by an uncaring tyrant.

The plot moves along, as we'd expect in a Cinderella story, toward its **climax** at the ambassador's reception. (Shaw originally omitted this scene because it was too expensive to produce onstage. In the musical *My Fair Lady* it is the climactic scene.) Meanwhile we watch the relationship between Eliza and Higgins develop. Actually Shaw shows us little or nothing of the training of Eliza, whereas in *My Fair Lady* it serves as the basis for a series of delightful songs.

The most obvious question raised by the play—can Higgins succeed in passing Eliza off as a duchess?—is answered when Eliza charms everyone at the reception. But the most important questions—what is to become of Eliza? and what is to become of the relationship between Higgins and Eliza?—are not answered until the last scene, when Shaw delivers his message—to our satisfaction or dissatisfaction.

A Myth

Pygmalion and Galatea
retold by Edith Hamilton

A gifted young sculptor of Cyprus, named Pygmalion, was a woman hater.

"Detesting the faults beyond measure which nature has given to women," he resolved never to marry. His art, he told himself, was enough for him. Nevertheless, the statue he made and devoted all his genius to was that of a woman. Either he could not dismiss what he so disapproved of from his mind as easily as from his life or else he was bent on forming a perfect woman and showing men the deficiencies of the kind they had to put up with.

However that was, he labored long and devotedly on the statue and produced a most exquisite work of art. But lovely as it was, he could not rest content. He kept on working at it, and daily under his skillful fingers it grew more beautiful. No woman ever born, no statue ever made, could approach it. When nothing could be added to its perfections, a strange fate had befallen its creator: he had fallen in love, deeply, passionately in love, with the thing he had made. It must be said in explanation that the statue did not look like a statue; no one would have thought it was ivory or stone, but warm human flesh, motionless for a moment only. Such was the wondrous power of this disdainful young man. The supreme achievement of art was his, the art of concealing art.

But from that time on, the sex he scorned had their revenge. No hopeless lover of a living maiden was ever so desperately unhappy as Pygmalion. He kissed those enticing lips—they could not kiss him back; he caressed her hands, her face—they were unresponsive; he took her in his arms—she remained a cold and passive form. For a time he tried to pretend, as children do with their toys. He would dress her in rich robes, trying the effect of one delicate or glowing color after another, and imagine she was pleased. He would bring her the gifts real maidens love, little birds and gay flowers and the shining tears of amber Phaëthon's sisters weep, and then dream that she thanked him with eager affection. He put her to bed at night and tucked her in all soft and warm, as little girls do their dolls. But he was not a child; he could not keep on pretending. In the end he gave up. He loved a lifeless thing, and he was utterly and hopelessly wretched.

This singular passion did not long remain concealed from the Goddess of Passionate Love. Venus was interested in something that seldom came her way, a new kind of lover, and she determined to help a young man who could be enamored and yet original.

The feast day of Venus was, of course, especially honored in Cyprus, the island which first received the goddess after she rose from the foam. Snow-white heifers whose horns had been gilded were offered in numbers to her; the heavenly odor of incense was spread through the island from her many altars; crowds thronged her temples; not an unhappy lover but was there with his gift, praying that his love might turn kind. There too, of course, was Pygmalion. He dared to ask the goddess only that he might find a maiden like his statue, but Venus knew what he really wanted, and as a sign that she favored his prayer, the flame on the altar he stood before leaped up three times, blazing into the air.

Very thoughtful at this good omen, Pygmalion sought his house and his love, the thing he had created and given his heart to. There she stood on her pedestal, entrancingly beautiful. He caressed her, and then he started back. Was it self-deception, or did she really feel warm to his touch? He kissed her lips, a long lingering kiss, and felt them grow soft beneath his. He touched her arms, her shoulders; their hardness vanished. It was like watching wax soften in the sun. He clasped her wrist; blood was pulsing there. Venus, he thought. This is the goddess's doing. And with unutterable gratitude and joy he put his arms around his love and saw her smile into his eyes and blush.

Venus herself graced their marriage with her presence, but what happened after that we do not know, except that Pygmalion named the maiden Galatea and that their son, Paphos, gave his name to Venus's favorite city.

A Musical Comedy

"The Rain in Spain"
from *My Fair Lady*
by Alan Jay Lerner

My Fair Lady: A Musical Comedy in Two Acts, *based on* Pygmalion *by George Bernard Shaw, with lyrics and libretto by Alan Jay Lerner and music by Frederick Loewe, opened on Broadway on March 15, 1956.*

Before this scene opens, Henry Higgins, a professor of phonetics, has encountered Eliza Doolittle, a cockney-speaking flower girl, and Colonel Pickering, an expert on Indian dialects. Higgins has made a wager with Pickering that, with six months of instruction, he can pass Eliza off as a duchess. Now Eliza and Pickering are living with Higgins in his house on Wimpole Street, where Higgins is hard at work correcting Eliza's speech and Pickering is offering encouragement. Higgins is browbeating Eliza; Pickering is urging him to go easy; Eliza is exhausted.

[*The lights come up in the study,* ELIZA *is on the stool in front of the desk.* HIGGINS *is in the alcove repairing a metronome.* PICKERING *as usual is in the wing chair reading the London Times.*]

Eliza. The rine in spine sties minely in the pline.
Higgins (*correcting her*). The rain in Spain stays mainly in the plain.
Eliza. Didn't I sy that?

Higgins. No, Eliza, you didn't "sy" that. You didn't even "say" that. (*He picks up a small burner and brings it down to the desk.*) Every night before you get into bed, where you used to say your prayers, I want you to repeat: "The rain in Spain stays mainly in the plain," fifty times. You will get much further with the Lord if you learn not to offend His ears. Now for your "H's." Pickering, this is going to be ghastly!

Pickering. Control yourself, Higgins. Give the girl a chance.

Higgins (*patiently*). Of course. No one expects her to get it right the first time. Watch closely, Eliza. (*He places the burner on the desk and lights the flame.*) You see this flame? Every time you say your aitch properly, the flame will waver. Every time you drop your aitch, the flame will remain stationary. That's how you will know you've done it correctly; in time your ear will hear the difference. Now, listen carefully; in Hertford, Hereford and Hampshire, hurricanes hardly ever happen.

[ELIZA *sits down behind the desk.*]

Now repeat after me, In Hertford, Hereford and Hampshire, hurricanes hardly ever happen.

Eliza (*conscientiously*). In 'ertford, 'ereford and 'ampshire 'urricanes 'ardly hever 'appen!

Higgins (*infuriated*). No, no, no, no! Have you no ear at all?

Eliza (*willingly*). Should I do it over?

Higgins. No. Please, no! We must start from the very beginning. (*He kneels before the flame.*) Do this: ha, ha, ha, ha. (*He rises.*)

Eliza. Ha–ha–ha–ha. (*She looks up at him happily.*)

Higgins. Well go on. Go on.

[ELIZA *continues,* HIGGINS *strolls casually over to* PICKERING, *leaving* ELIZA *to aspirate at the flame.*]

Does the same thing hold true in India, Pickering; the peculiar habit of not only dropping a letter like the letter aitch, but using it where it shouldn't be? Like "hever" instead of "ever"? You'll notice some of the Slavic peoples when they learn to speak English have a tendency to that with their G's. They say "linger" (soft g) instead of "linger" (hard g); and then they turn around and say "singer" (hard g) instead of "singer" (soft g).

[PICKERING *had never thought about it and naturally is perplexed.*]

I wonder why that's so. I must look it up.

[HIGGINS *starts for the landing.* ELIZA, *by this time, is sinking fast from lack of oxygen.* PICKERING *notices her dying gasps and pulls* HIGGINS' *arm to call his attention to it.*]

(*Thinking which book to consult*) Go on! Go on!

[*He continues up the stairs.* ELIZA *musters together one final "HA" and blows out the flame. The room is plunged into darkness.*]

[*The lights come up in the study.* PICKERING *is seated in his favorite chair with a large and fulsome tea table before him.* ELIZA *is on the sofa.* HIGGINS *is standing by the xylophone, a cup in one hand, a xylophone mallet in the other. He taps out eight notes. "How kind of you to let me come."*]

Higgins. *Kind* of you, *kind* of you, *kind* of you. Now listen, Eliza. (*He plays them again.*) How kind of you to let me come.
Eliza. How kind of *you* to let me come.
Higgins (*puts down the mallet in despair and walks over to the tea table*). No! *Kind* of you. It's just like "*cup* of tea." *Kind* of you—*cup* of tea. *Kind* of you—Say "cup of tea."
Eliza (*hungrily*). Cappatea.
Higgins. No! No! A cup of tea . . . (*Takes a mouthful of cake from the tray*) It's awfully good cake. I wonder where Mrs. Pearce gets it?

Pickering. Mmmmm! First rate! The strawberry tarts are delicious. And did you try the pline cake? (HIGGINS *looks at him in horror and then turns to* ELIZA.)

Higgins. Now, try it again, Eliza. A cup of tea. A cup of tea.

Eliza (*longingly*). A cappatea.

Higgins. Can't you hear the difference? Put your tongue forward until it squeezes against the top of your lower teeth. Now say "cup."

Eliza (*her attention only on the cake in* HIGGINS' *hand*). C-cup.

Higgins. Now say "of."

Eliza. Of.

Higgins. Now say, cup, cup, cup, cup—of, of, of, of.

Eliza. Cup, cup, cup, cup—of, of, of, of! Cup, cup, cup, cup—of, of, of, of . . .

Pickering (*as she's practicing*). By Jove, that was a glorious tea, Higgins. Do finish the strawberry tart. I couldn't eat another thing.

Higgins. No, thanks, old chap, really.

Pickering. It's a shame to waste it.

Higgins. Oh it won't go to waste. (*He takes the last tart.*) I know someone who's immensely fond of strawberry tarts.

[ELIZA's *eyes light up hopefully. But alas,* HIGGINS *walks right past her and goes to the bird cage.*]

Higgins (*pushing the cake thru the bars*). *Cheep, cheep, cheep!*

Eliza (*shrieking*). Aaaaaaaaaaaooooooooowwww!!

Blackout

[*The lights come up again in the study.* ELIZA *is seated in the wing chair.* HIGGINS *has drawn up the stool and is facing her, a small box of marbles in his hand. He is placing them in her mouth.*]

Higgins. Four . . . five . . . six marbles. There we are. (*He holds up a slip of paper.*) Now, I want you to read this and enunciate each word just as if the marbles were not in your mouth. "With blackest moss, the flower pots were thickly crusted, one and all." Each word clear as a bell. (*He gives her the paper.*)

Eliza (*unintelligibly*). With blackest moss the flower pots . . . I can't! I can't!

Pickering (*from the sofa*). I say, Higgins, are those pebbles really necessary?

Higgins. If they were necessary for Demosthenes,° they are necessary for Eliza Doolittle. Go on, Eliza.

Eliza (*trying again with no better results*). With blackest moss, the flower pots were thickly crusted, one and all. . . .

Higgins. I cannot understand a word. Not a word.

Eliza (*her anger coming thru the marbles and "flower pots"*). With blackest moss, the flower pots were thickly crusted, one and all; the rusted nails fell from the knots that held the pear to the gable-wall . . .

Pickering (*soon after she has begun*). I say, Higgins, perhaps the poem is too difficult for the girl. Why don't you try a simpler one, like: "The Owl and the Pussycat"? Oh, yes, that's a charming one.

Higgins (*bellowing*). Pickering! I cannot hear the girl!

[ELIZA *gasps and takes the marbles out of her mouth.*]

What's the matter? Why did you stop?

Eliza. I swallowed one.

Higgins (*reassuringly*). Oh, don't worry. I have plenty more. Open your mouth.

°**Demosthenes** (384–322 B.C.): a great Greek orator who is said to have overcome a speech impediment by speaking with pebbles in his mouth.

[*The lights go out.*]

[*The lights come up again on the study.* ELIZA *is draped wearily on the sofa.* PICKERING *is half asleep in the wing chair.* HIGGINS *is seated at his desk, an ice-bag on his head. The gray light outside the windows indicates the early hours of the morning.*]

Higgins (*wearily*). The rain in Spain stays mainly in the plain.
Eliza. I can't. I'm so tired. I'm so tired.
Pickering (*half asleep*). Oh, for God's sake, Higgins. It must be three o'clock in the morning. Do be reasonable.
Higgins (*rising*). I am always reasonable. Eliza, If I can go on with a blistering headache, you can.
Eliza. I have a headache, too.
Higgins. Here.

[*He plops the ice-bag on her head. She takes it off her head and buries her face in her hands, exhausted to the point of tears.*]

(*With sudden gentleness.*) Eliza, I know you're tired. I know your head aches. I know your nerves are as raw as meat in a butcher's window. But think what you're trying to accomplish. (*He sits next to her on the sofa.*) Think what you're dealing with. The majesty and grandeur of the English language. It's the greatest possession we have. The noblest sentiments that ever flowed in the hearts of men are contained in its extraordinary, imaginative and musical mixtures of sounds. That's what you've set yourself to conquer, Eliza. And conquer it you will. (*He rises, goes to the chair behind his desk and seats himself heavily.*) Now, try it again.
Eliza (*slowly*). The rain in Spain stays mainly in the plain.
Higgins (*sitting up*). What was that?

Eliza. The rain in Spain stays mainly in the plain.

Higgins (*rising, unbelievably*). Again.

Eliza. The rain in Spain stays mainly in the plain.

Higgins (*to* PICKERING). I think she's got it! I think she's got it!

A News Feature

from Speaking Across the Divide
by John Lahr

The internationally famous Juilliard School, located in New York City, offers college degrees in music, dance, and drama. This article focuses on two teenagers from Harlem who attended a special speech class at Juilliard. The goal of the class is to help intelligent and gifted inner-city high school students move beyond the limitations that might have been imposed on them by their dialects. Their Henry Higgins is Denise Woods, an African American actress and singer on the faculty of Juilliard's Drama Division. Like Eliza Doolittle, Woods's students learn to "[strip] away the vocal habits of their environment"—without sacrificing their own "voice."

After speech class last spring at the Juilliard School, just across the street from the white marble towers of high culture at Lincoln Center, it was the custom of Yasmin Moya-Gutierrez and Tanasha Bennett, two talented, college-bound citizens of Harlem, to take the subway home. The actual journey is about four miles, but the distance between worlds is much greater. When they stepped off the subway and into the bright, disheveled uptown day, they were entering not just a different community but a different community of speech. Yasmin and Tanasha are both, in that sense, bilingual; they know that they must simultaneously be cool and defeat cool as they maneuver through the gantlet of street talk, which in some quarters these days goes under the name of Ebonics. As Yasmin, a svelte Dominican girl of eighteen who has studied dance at Jacques D'Amboise's National Dance Institute and at the Alvin Ailey American Dance Center, bustles through her Latino turf, around 135th Street and Broadway, everything about her—her handsome face, her upright posture, her purposeful walk—is pitched against the prevailing lackadaisical uptown style, which, she tells me, she finds "bovine."

"I hear people yelling through megaphones about the sales going on in their bodegas," she says. "I hear guys trying to talk to a girl: 'Hey, baby!' 'Hey, Mami!' 'So many curves and me without brakes!'" Yasmin, who graduated last June from the Bronx High School of Science, scored in the top 15 percent nationally on her SATs, and is now a member of Bryn Mawr's class of 2000, doesn't "hang": her schedule was usually "from my house to school, from school to dance class to work to speech class." Yasmin stands apart from the street culture whose commotion surrounds her. "When I first heard 'It's brick outside,' I did not know what that was," she admits. "It means real cold. People would be like, 'Yo, man, it's freakin' brick.' And I'd be like, 'Brick? OK, red?'"

Tanasha, on the other hand, a seventeen-year-old African American with short-cropped hair and a bounce in her step, who attends Brooklyn Tech, faces down the street talk with what she calls her "nobody-can-beat-me attitude." As she explains it, "Can't nobody beat me. Can't nobody do anything to me. Because somebody's always gonna try to challenge me." And somebody always does. When she walks through her stomping ground, on 151st Street between Broadway and Amsterdam, the Dominican guys holler, "Girl, speak!"

She explains, "If I don't answer, it's always 'You can't speak to me now? *Tu fea!*' They think I don't know what it means. It means 'ugly.' I keep on going." Tanasha's way of adapting to her dangerous terrain is to become fierce herself. "Uptown, I'm evil," Tanasha says, following the street practice of changing or inverting meanings, like "evil" for "rude," "bad" for "cool," "dope" for "great." "Say for instance, I'm walking down 135th Street. All you hear is 'Yo, Shorty. Can I get you numbah? Waz'a deal wi'choo?'—yada-yada-yada. Everybody yelling at you. Trying to talk to you. And my face: I don't smile. I'm walking. Just leave me alone. Don't bother me. That's the image I'm trying to portray. I just change. I harden myself. People don't seem to get that. They try to talk to me anyway. 'Yo, Shorty. Put a smile on yo' face, it's not that bad a day.'" She adds, "Downtown, people don't bother you." Tanasha doesn't tell her uptown friends about her speech class at Juilliard. "In a different environment, I'm dealing with a different kind of people, so I act accordingly," she says. She enjoys black vernacular and understands why it's so pervasive uptown. "We feel more unified. We have our own thing," she says. "It makes us feel stronger together—the fact that we can talk in a way that other people wouldn't understand." But she also sees the limitations of her uptown dialect. "If I only knew slang, how far could I get? I couldn't do anything but live in Harlem, be successful in Harlem. I don't think these people realize that."

In Room 312, a large, sunny rectangular rehearsal hall at Juilliard, Yasmin and Tanasha lie on their backs with their heads side by side. Tanasha's white Nikes are drawn up under her, her knees bent; Yasmin's sandaled feet, even in repose, are in second position. Along with ten other teenage students, they are breathing deeply—or, more exactly, they are stripping away the vocal habits of their environment to find their breath and their natural voices. Their eyes are shut. The ozone around them is filled with mellifluous directions from their voice coach,

Denise Woods, who is saying "Now, breathe with your ribs. Not your chest. Not your chest. Just your ribs. So that you're really feeling the origin of this voice, which is breath."

Spirit has its root in the Latin for "to breathe," and the course, which is called Express Yourself! is itself an act of inspiration. The students are learning how to give proper volume, depth, and articulation to their voices, in order to put their spirits effectively into the world. Once a week, for an entire fall or spring semester (this particular session ran from January to June), the class assembles for two hours after school to identify and to eradicate such strange-sounding chronic maladies as "wet *t*s," "muddy consonants," "tone endings," and "diphthong abuse"—the miscues of pronunciation that, once the youngsters venture outside the circumscribed world of Harlem, imperceptibly chip away at their life chances. "A woman who utters such depressing and disgusting sounds has no right to be anywhere—no right to live," Henry Higgins, the upper-class English professor of phonetics, says in George Bernard Shaw's *Pygmalion* on first hearing Eliza Doolittle's cockney sludge. Shaw saw speech as the bulwark of class division. "It is impossible for an Englishman to open his mouth without making some other Englishman despise him," he said. Money talks, as the saying goes: A nebulous voice with poor pronunciation broadcasts impoverishment; it lacks credibility and can't be heard. So how can minorities, who grow up outside the mainstream, translate themselves into it without, like Eliza, simply mimicking the sound and manners of the dominant class?

As Yasmin, Tanasha, and the other students breathe in and expel an *s* sound up to the ceiling, they are addressing the problem. They are nearly as old as Eliza Doolittle but share nothing with her except ghettoized speech. Unlike Eliza, whose choice in static Edwardian society was to sell flowers in the gutter or sell herself through a society marriage, they are part of a mobile, multicultural America and have ambitions to find their way on their own terms, as surgeons, engineers, lawyers, psychologists, teachers. They are members of a select group, whose intellectual ambitions have been encouraged by the Harlem Educational Activities Fund, or HEAF, a tax-exempt public charity that provides Harlem junior high students with tutorial services and continues to bolster their progress in high school, mentoring them and arranging special trips and enrichment classes like Express Yourself!, as well as supporting them once they get to college, with a special 800 number and money to come home on holidays. The program works with eight schools, including the Asa Philip Randolph School for the Humanities (P.S. 76, on West 121st Street), which had the lowest literacy rate in the city—nine percent—when HEAF first approached it, five years ago; that figure has since risen to twenty-one percent. HEAF also works with Mott Hall, a "selective" public junior high, near the campus of City College, at Convent Avenue and 131st Street, which both Yasmin and Tanasha attended.

They and other gifted students have the intelligence and the ambition to move beyond their community, but they may not yet possess the vocal or presentational skills that would enable them to move comfortably between worlds. This became transparent a couple of years ago to the real estate developer and philanthropist Daniel Rose, who is the founder and president of HEAF, while he was watching an awards ceremony for high achievers in HEAF's Support Net Program, which over the last seven years has helped several hundred students get into rigorous academic high schools and then apply to college. As the students were called to receive their plaques from General George Price, the handsome, ramrod-straight brother of the singer Leontyne Price, Rose realized that "they didn't know how to come up and get the award." He recalls, "The body language was the tentative body language of someone who didn't belong, a mixture of pride and embarrassment. I thought, Some of these kids have only a year before they're off to college. How are they going to look at their Harvard interview? I don't want anyone to put them down. I want them to feel self-confident. I want their body language to say 'I'm here by right—not by sufferance. I'm comfortable here.'" Over dinner that evening, Rose worried aloud about the problem to Gloria Levitas, an anthropologist and the wife of Mitchel Levitas, then the editor of the Times Op-Ed page. She suggested acting lessons for the kids. The next day, Rose was on the phone to Joseph Polisi, the head of Juilliard, and a week later Polisi brought Denise Woods to Rose. "We met. You can't help but fall in love with her," says Rose, who gave Woods a free hand to invent a course. "She's like an actress creating her role."

The offer came at the right moment for Woods, a buoyant, cosmopolitan thirty-nine-year-old African American actress and singer who, like her students, started life as a project girl—in her case, in a predominantly Jewish neighborhood on the Lower East Side, at the foot of the Williamsburg Bridge. "I *tawked* like this *awl* the *toime.* I kid you not," says Woods, who was Miss Black Teen America in 1972, got her BFA in theater from Juilliard in 1979, and joined the voice-and-speech faculty of the Drama Division at her alma mater in 1993—the first female African American drama instructor in Juilliard's history. "I felt that at Juilliard I was working in an ivory tower," she says. "I wanted to take what I had and give it to some black folks because, God knows, we needed it." For a while, in 1994, Woods was the speech coach for professional athletes, like Carlton Bailey of the New York Giants and Alex English, former star of the Denver Nuggets. "I was watching these amazing athletes, but once I heard them speak, I couldn't take them seriously," she says. "I felt that they had a responsibility to be well-rounded role models. They had economic power, but they had no communication tools—the power to win people over." What defeated Woods's short-lived project with the athletes was a lack of what has made her HEAF speech class such a success: the athletes, who were already rich and famous, didn't have the will to do the work, while the kids, whose talents are still in the embryo stage, as Woods explains, "are primed for it."

When she inaugurated the class, in January 1996, the students' presentational problems were glaring. "They didn't quite feel good enough about themselves," Woods says. "They didn't sit up, breathe, and speak. Personality was very much masked." Berthsy Ayide, Julisa Herrera, Yamilett Pichardo, Amarilis Cespedes, and Yesenia Michel talked with high, strangulated, nasal voices; Miguel Vargas, Qiuwei Chen, and Johan Yege spoke almost in whispers; Jennifer Jahorie was squeaky; Ruobing Wang was breathy, and her shyness was a formidable barrier to communication. Tanasha was all volume and attitude, and Yasmin, the group's only high school senior, had a lot to say but said it in a monotone.

Woods's idea is not to remake her students. "Certainly you cannot sacrifice your own voice," she says, reflecting on her personal struggle to assimilate as a college student. "I came into an environment where people were truly educated, and I felt intimidated. I felt less than. I felt as if I needed to catch up. I got this wonderful hodgepodge of culture that this world-renowned place was offering me. But somehow I lost the black girl who was from the Lower East Side, who was just as important as the artist. There was no one there to tell me that this element of my being was just as important as Denise the artist." It took Woods ten years to reclaim her black identity. "I felt I couldn't bring that to the table," Woods says. "There was no place for it." Now, thirty years later, there is a place. Woods frequently tells the class, "I don't want you to take this technique and become someone else. I want you to find *you*."

Woods's class is not a charm school but a kind of laboratory for multicultural living—for inhabiting that liminal zone between cultures which increasingly defines the American cultural experience. "I'm just giving you options," Woods tells the students. "That's all. I don't want you to be stuck in one style." About Tanasha, for instance, whom she calls "a sassy mama," Woods says, "She's this girl from the 'hood. She brings all these wonderful inflections that are her, that are beautiful. That I don't want to touch, because that's Tanasha. As long as she can be understood, as long as she's audible—that's all I want." When Woods was coming of age, the prevailing image of American assimilation was "the melting pot," a distillation of all cultures into one homogeneous mass. In the intervening decades of racial dialogue, "the melting pot" has evolved into "the salad bowl," where the ingredients mix but also retain their separate qualities.

—from *The New Yorker,*
January 27, 1997